REACHING
TOWARD
EASTER

12.

REACHING TOWARD EASTER

DEVOTIONS *for* LENT

DEREK MAUL

UPPER
ROOM BOOKS®
NASHVILLE

The Upper Room Web site: www.upperroom.org

UPPER ROOM®, UPPER ROOM BOOKS®, and design logos are trademarks owned by The Upper Room®, a ministry of GBOD®, Nashville, Tennessee. All rights reserved.

Unless otherwise indicated, scripture quotations are from the New Revised Standard Version Bible, copyright © 1989 National Council of the Churches of Christ in the United States of America. Used by permission. All rights reserved.

Scripture quotations marked (KJV) are from the King James Version.

Scripture quotations marked (NIV) are taken from THE HOLY BIBLE, NEW INTERNATIONAL VERSION®, NIV® Copyright © 1973, 1978, 1984, 2011 by Biblica, Inc.™ Used by permission. All rights reserved worldwide.

Scripture quotations marked (NLT) are taken from the Holy Bible, New Living Translation, copyright © 1996, 2004, 2007. Used by permission of Tyndale House Publishers, Inc., Carol Stream, Illinois 60188. All rights reserved.

Cover images: © Getty Images
Cover design: Bruce Gore | Gore Studio, Inc.
Interior design: PerfecType, Nashville, TN
Printed in the United States of America

Library of Congress Cataloging-in-Publication Data

Maul, Derek, 1956-
    Reaching toward Easter: devotions for Lent / by Derek Maul.
        p. cm.
    ISBN 978-0-8358-1061-6
    1. Lent—Prayers and devotions. I. Title.
    BV85.M3755 2011
    242'.34—dc23
                                        2011021260

To Rebekah
This life we have built together continues to teach me more about the
gracious, openhearted, generous love of God than any resource I have
ever come across. So I'm dedicating this book to you because you are
my inspiration, my heart, and the most profound explanation of what it
means to live faith—and love—out loud.

ACKNOWLEDGMENTS

The idea for this book first came up in a conversation with Robin Pippin at a book expo in Indianapolis on a cold January day; so thanks to Robin for blowing on the embers a few years later when my own, personal Reaching Toward Easter experience began to translate into a manuscript. Since that time the project has taken shape in response to the belief of many good people. So I acknowledge the spiritual gift of discernment via Robin, Eli Fisher, Anne Trudel, and Joanna Bradley at Upper Room Books; the gift of encouragement in my best friend Gerard and my co-teacher Charles Willard, and via the gifted and spiritually astute Praise Band at First Presbyterian Church of Brandon; and — most poignantly — the gift of inspirational via the amazing preaching of my wife and pastor, Rebekah Maul.

TABLE OF CONTENTS

FRESH EYES ON EASTER

John 12 opens with the words, "Six days before the Passover Jesus came to Bethany, the home of Lazarus, whom he had raised from the dead. There they gave a dinner for him" (verses 1-2).

Martha served; Mary anointed; Judas got upset about the extravagance; Jesus hinted about his upcoming death; and the religious authorities plotted. The very next day Jesus arrived at the city of Jerusalem, and he entered as if the kingdom had already been established. Events rushed headlong toward crucifixion.

That week, on a Thursday evening, Jesus shared one last, unforgettable dinner with his friends. There was a lot to talk about, a lot to get ready for, and a lot to digest. Jesus' passion is loaded with life-charged meaning, lessons and ideas that it's critical we think about if our observance of Easter is to have the life-charged, long-term impact for which Jesus gave everything to make possible.

The season of Lent is about preparation, so that we can "Enter [God's] gates with thanksgiving, and his courts with praise" (Ps. 100:4) with the quality of renewed spiritual energy that comes in response to the sacred rhythms of daily observance. Easter celebrates the victory of light over darkness and the reality of the kingdom Christ invites us to explore.

But Easter, like Christmas, has fallen victim to our cultural penchant for sucking meaning from significant Christian holidays and replacing that meaning with tawdry values borrowed from the secular world, values rooted in consumerism and humanism and our incessant demand to be entertained.

We routinely adapt our faith and practices to fit more neatly into the cultural norm, rather than inviting Jesus to be the catalyst for change both in and through our lives. As a result, we often arrive at Good Friday having missed the focused opportunity Lent provides to share in the original disciples' experiences of sitting at table with Jesus; walking the dusty path from Bethany to the very gates of Jerusalem, observing Jesus; and listening closely to his words of grace and hope and challenge.

This book offers a devotional pilgrimage through Lent, using the framework of John's narrative as a daily guide. Together we'll journey from Ash Wednesday through Holy Week, on to Resurrection Sunday, and then to the challenge for the rest of our lives—the challenge to live as "Easter People" in the real world.

Try to read one day at a time. Pray with me at the end of each chapter; invite a friend or two to join you along the way. Let's not miss the rich blessing that God has in store for us.

Grace and peace—DEREK MAUL

Day One: Tuesday

SACRED RHYTHM

Read John 8:31-33.

If you continue in my word, you are truly my disciples (v. 31).

I couldn't help but notice the gaudy flyer taped across the glass entry at my favorite grocery store. "Easter," the handbill confidently announced, "Is On Aisle 13."

Curious, I walked around to take a look. But I was disappointed from the outset.

Aisle 13 was overrun with fuzzy stuffed bunnies—pale blue, pink, white, aqua, and an obscure kind of mauve. Next, I found candy, enough to keep several dental offices busy well into the summer. There were greetings cards too, sporting messages such as "Hoppy Easter" and "Egg-static We're Friends!" Baskets, ribbons, toys, and various hollow plastic eggs rounded out the display.

I felt tricked, victim of another bait-and-switch tactic by the advertisers. There wasn't the slightest hint of a faith-based Easter anywhere on Aisle 13.

The authentic theme of Easter is diametric—both beautiful and horrific at the same time. If we are going to acknowledge the season at all, it's imperative that we consider the complete picture:

- Life by definition assumes death
- Victory suggests the possibility of defeat
- Peace involves the understanding that conflict exists
- Resurrection presupposes crucifixion
- Good grasps the fact of evil
- Right often requires a daring stand in the face of wrong

Much about our world is spoiled by fear. The Easter story recognizes that truth, faces the dread with courage, and emerges in a triumph that simply cannot be appropriately celebrated outside some understanding of freedom's tremendous cost.

The story of Easter is the story of Jesus—an itinerant rabbi, a carpenter from the small town of Nazareth—who was a real man: God in the flesh living love and goodness out loud. He died on Good Friday, a slow, agonizing, public torture designed by Rome to demonstrate the immediate and terrible consequences of disrupting the brutal *Pax Romana*, the peace of Rome. The notice tacked above the Savior's head could easily have read: "Dangerous Freethinker," "Radical," or "This man violated the status quo."

But Jesus' idea of freedom was problematic for more than just Rome; it disturbed many of his fellow Israelites too. Jesus failed to fulfill the "Conquering Warrior Hero" concept or to deliver the political freedom they sought. He spent three years explaining and clarifying what he meant by the phrase "kingdom of God," but the crowds kept looking for something more familiar.

Today, like those early followers, we still tend to reinvent the character and the picture of the God we worship, so the image fits more tidily with the values and the priorities that define the culture in which we are comfortable. In truth, the huge win Jesus achieved at Easter still calls for us to reject the trap of the status quo. It is a W over greed; selfishness; religiosity; and the entire me-first, consumer-driven mentality that illustrates our foundational cultural malfunction. But it's easier to replace the scandal of the Cross with a basket of candy and less taxing when we focus on the traditions of springtime rather than an empty tomb. We'd rather not think too much about the heavy price paid for the freedom we take so lightly.

The bottom line is that we're not going to find Easter on Aisle 13! And we're not going to find it at all unless we are prepared to talk about the meaning of the Cross. Jesus walked into all of this with eyes wide open and a heart full to overflowing with a generous and heroic love for our world. This life is a journey, and I want to walk this section of the path with my eyes open too, with the Prince of Peace walking at my side.

SACRED RHYTHM

Growing up, my favorite thing about the season of Lent was Shrove Tuesday, the last day before our acts of self-denial set in for the long haul. Back in

England we simply called it "Pancake Day." Later, living on the Gulf Coast of Florida, I learned about the term "Fat Tuesday." But, sitting around my mother's kitchen table as a hungry ten-year-old, I didn't care what they called it, so long as she served up her amazing English-style pancakes, rich crepes floating in lemon juice and sugar. My brother and I tore into them like there was no tomorrow.

Of course that was the original idea of Fat Tuesday. There really was no tomorrow so far as indulgence was concerned, not until Easter, well over six weeks down the road. But I grew up in a vigorously Protestant household, and I can't recall any particular Lenten uptick in our spiritual practices; at least not until the short run from Palm Sunday through Good Friday and into Easter morning.

I have since come to believe that a thoughtful observance of the spiritual calendar, a kind of sacred rhythm, has a lot of merit in a world that has become so overbearingly secular. I want to invite us all to share in this devotional journey to "continue in [Christ's] word" and to develop a sacred rhythm. I want us to be prepared to understand the meaning of the Cross.

At the start of this journey, I invite you to contemplate the ways that you have experienced the message of the Cross fitting into the message of the spiritual calendar.

Prayer: You are both the guide and the destination, gracious God. Please grant each one of us the blessing of Divine Presence as we journey through Lent. Amen.

LIGHT AND THE DISPOSITION OF LIFE

Read John 12:1-19.

Six days before the Passover Jesus came to Bethany, the home of Lazarus, whom he had raised from the dead. There they gave a dinner for him. Martha served, and Lazarus was one of those at the table with him (vv. 1-2).

Rebekah and I tell the following story from our epic trip "out West," back when Andrew and Naomi were still snarky teens. We drove from Tampa all the way to Colorado and beyond, 6,800 miles over three weeks.

One day, in the middle of the Rocky Mountains, we signed up for one of those "abandoned gold mine" tours. The train took us a half-mile into the heart of the mountain. Eventually we came into contact with darkness on a level I had never experienced before. Our guide turned off all the lights until there was just one remaining. Then he stood on a chair.

"Close your eyes and put your hand two inches in front of your face," the guide said. "Keep them closed. Now I'm going to turn out the single remaining light, and I want you to open your eyes after I count to three."

The result was shocking. Not only could we not see our hands in front of our faces, we could see absolutely nothing at all. It was as if matter no longer existed, just sound, and there wasn't much of that because we were all almost too nervous to even breathe.

About thirty seconds later—an extremely long time in those conditions—our guide told us all to hold perfectly still and to be completely quiet because he was going to light a small wooden match. When he did, the effect was amazing; we could see everything! We were in a cavern about the size of a three-hundred-seat auditorium, but there wasn't a cubic foot of the space that did not experience at least some degree of illumination.

Well, he got the "Wow!" element he was looking for. The tour was a definite success. Nobody found a smidgen of gold, but we didn't care and we all went on our way happy. But my mind could not stop working as I thought about the effect that even one small spark of light will always have on darkness. As the Gospel of John says, "The light shines in the darkness, and the darkness can never extinguish it" (NLT).

Here's the really cool part. Even though the wooden match produced "artificial" light, it turns out that the phosphorescent energy that illuminated our cavern was still a conduit for the power of the sun's energy, which is absorbed, stored, recalibrated, reconstituted, unearthed, transformed, packaged, repackaged, and ultimately released via a thousand different pathways.

We are all called to play the part of the match in the dark cave that is this world. In the beginning of John's Gospel there's a telling passage about our critical role as conduits for the light. "There came a man who was sent from God; his name was John. He came as a witness to testify concerning that light" (John 1:6-7, NIV).

If there's an ounce of hope in this world, if there's any impulse to growth, if we understand any sense of urgency beyond merely existing—then that's the quality of light John was talking about in his testimony. Life and light testify to the truth about creation.

LENT CALLS TO THE PROMISE OF RESURRECTION

The promise inherent in springtime runs deep. During my childhood in England, February was the time that the green tips of crocus leaves pushed their way through the slush of freezing rain or the residue of melting snow, insistent on a cold, wet, uninviting morning. I'd be outside, under protest, with our enthusiastic golden retriever and there the flowers would be, little heads poking up with extravagant hope. "We can do it!" they seemed to taunt. "What's your excuse!"

Today, living in Florida, I find that springtime is already in full bloom in February. Everywhere the garden pushes ahead in response to the imperative of life—the dynamic life force resident in the cell structure of even the simplest plant; the impulse not just to live but also to grow; unrelenting life.

The power that created—and still creates—is best described as the author and the sustainer of life. Separation from the Creator is best described as death—life set aside in favor of darkness. But my journey as a follower of Jesus has given me this new disposition, and that is the disposition of life.

A surge of vitality comes through cold soil and dead wood every spring. Such animation just hints at the brilliant life offered through the process of birth and resurrection. Jesus put it this way, when he was talking with a man named Nicodemus: "Do not be astonished that I said to you, 'You must be born from above'" (John 3:7).

"See, I am making all things new" (Rev. 21:5).

Newness; springtime; hope beyond winter; resurrection; all of nature shouting instruction to each one of us in terms of our journey. Time to ask myself some questions:

- In what ways am I allowing the Spirit to work newness in me?
- How is my faith able to comprehend—in a fresh way—the promise of renewal?
- In what ways do I present the kind of evidence that the crocus demonstrates every year?
- How does the way that I live communicate the reality of God's amazing love to the world around me?

"So if anyone is in Christ, there is a new creation; everything old has passed away; see, everything has become new!" (2 Cor. 5:17).

Lazarus, who enjoyed dinner with Jesus in Bethany, was a new creation in Christ. And the story told every spring via re-creation points to the truth about the character of the Author of Creation. This journey together through Lent serves as an invitation to align the heart of our spiritual nature with the regenerative heart of God, the Sustainer and Deliverer, to set our intention toward life and to align ourselves with the light.

Examine your own life in light of the questions listed above.

Prayer: Accompany us on this journey to the Cross, Creator God. Sustain us by your Spirit; walk by our side; re-create us in the context of your awesome love. Amen.

Day Three: Thursday

AN ELEGANT, UNCOMPROMISING INVITATION TO LIVE

Read John 12:20-50.

> *"Now my soul is troubled. And what should I say—'Father, save me from this hour'? No, it is for this reason that I have come to this hour. Father, glorify your name." Then a voice came from heaven, "I have glorified it, and I will glorify it again" (vv. 27-28).*

Jesus was troubled. Not regarding the big picture. I imagine that he was crystal clear regarding the part he was destined to play in the unfolding story of redemption. But he was uneasy breathing this divine clarity yet living in and through the very mortal body of a human being, 100 percent God, 100 percent human. Jesus knew what was coming and the knowledge had to have introduced a level of dissonance that was, in a way, excruciating.

TROUBLED ON PURPOSE

One of the most remarkable truths about Jesus' journey to the Cross is the understanding that this was a deliberate, volitional act. Jesus made a purposeful, informed choice with his eyes wide open. Jesus knowingly stepped out, away from the table of admiring friends in Bethany, and turned his face toward Jerusalem. Jesus walked, one step at a time, in the direction of humiliation and the torturous death that he knew was waiting for him.

But why? Why close down the "founder as teacher" genius of the operation after only three years of active ministry? Why did Jesus stroll into the maelstrom at that particular time? Were there not still signs and wonders waiting to be performed? Were there not more disciples to make? Didn't the

Lord have more towns to visit, new people to tend to, and additional wisdom to speak?

Well, the answer to all these questions is yes. And the solution stares right back at us every time we look in the mirror. We have been commissioned to do these things as faithful Jesus followers in this twenty-first century. There's much more to do in our world today than there ever was at the time of Jesus. We are the hands and the feet and the compassion of Christ; we are the presence; we are the body. We are the proof—or otherwise—of the power that this message holds.

But Jesus had a particular and specific mission, clearly defined within the parameters of time and space. He laid out the essential message and left nothing to add in terms of the spoken word. Because, at the heart of it all, the point Jesus made is simple and pure; it is uncomplicated and direct. The gospel message is an elegant, uncompromising invitation to live.

After three years Jesus had communicated the essence of his vision clearly. But from the moment he died and for two thousand years since, his followers—that would include you and me—have been complicating every word and confusing every nuance until the heart of the gospel has far too often become almost unrecognizable! So I don't believe there was any more essential truth for Jesus to reveal, any more explanation for him to voice. Our opportunity is to go out there and get busy. And Jesus demonstrated the doing part with unequaled eloquence and profundity.

How did Jesus achieve this? "Having loved his own who were in the world, he loved them to the end" (John 13:1). The NIV puts the verse this way: "He now showed them the full extent of his love" by traveling to Jerusalem to face certain execution and ultimately to demonstrate the victory of light and life over darkness and death.

But Jesus had to turn his face; he had to set his will; and he had to take the first in a series of very deliberate steps.

Our first step is to examine our intention. Approximately forty days from now we're going to gather in some church building with believers and those on the periphery of faith and the curious to celebrate Jesus' Triumphal Entry into Jerusalem on Palm Sunday, the event that kicks off Holy Week.

But the question that's facing each one of us today is this: "Will I be ready?" What happens during the next six and a half weeks will determine how well prepared we are to take any kind of a journey with Jesus.

We may be invited to wave, cheer, and shout "Hosanna!" as the children lead the way with their palm branches. But somewhere down the road there's also the chance that following Jesus will eventually lead to some kind of cross. Today, think about what that may mean. And let's add commitment to our intention and so be on our way.

Prayer: Creator of all life, help us to set our sights and our intentions clearly on Jerusalem. Accompany us on our journey. Feed our souls. Grant us the strength to follow you no matter where the road leads. Amen.

GOING OVER THE HIGHLIGHTS ONE MORE TIME

Read John 13:1-20.

> *Jesus answered, "You do not know now what I am doing, but later you will understand" (v. 7).*

Sometimes the crowds surrounding Jesus were dense; very often his closest friends were fairly dense too. Same word, entirely different meaning.

Most evenings when our children were growing up, my wife and I would pepper our family dinner time conversation with questions. We found that to be a great way to coax ideas and opinions and honesty from the children, especially when they were teens. The practice worked so well that quite often I still go to dinner with friends or family armed with two or three guaranteed conversation starters in my hip-pocket, just in case.

Jesus was well known for doing the same kind of thing with his friends. His most frequent and telling questions went like this:

- 🕊 "Do you not understand?"

- 🕊 "Have you not seen and heard?"

- 🕊 "Don't you get it?"

- 🕊 "Are you not a student of the law?"

- 🕊 "Didn't your mother teach you anything . . . ?"

Not really, I made that one up! But the Gospel writers did often include phrases like, "And Jesus wondered at their lack of understanding" (see Matt. 15:16 and Mark 7:18).

Yet Jesus persisted. The great Teacher taught, rephrased, told parables, and lived by example. But his style of teaching was so foreign, so radical and so personal, to the way they were used to considering God. It was an approach markedly unusual in a harsh world where life was often dirt-cheap and the last thing anyone expected of a deity was compassion.

Many of them were, after all, looking for a political Messiah who would smash Rome into tiny pieces and establish a tangible kingdom of raw power. But instead, here was Jesus, walking on the water, turning water into wine, calming the storm, caring for children, touching lepers, and speaking with— of all the nerve—outcasts and women.

"The kingdom of God is like," he would say, and go on to startle his friends and followers with a story about a grain of seed, a lost sheep, or a merchant. And Jesus cared passionately for individuals. "Not even one common sparrow falls to the ground," he told anyone who was willing to listen, "without it mattering to God" (Matt. 10:29, author paraphrase).

Jesus got up from the table in Bethany, where he had been comfortable and loved and cared for, and made his way along the dusty road toward his irreversible fate in Jerusalem.

NON SEQUITUR

And so the ragtag band of Jesus-people entered the Holy City, triumphant at last and with their leader perched on the back of a borrowed donkey. It was an obvious sign of intent and a visible declaration of peace.

But Jesus failed to capitalize on the parade—at least in the way his friends expected. He refused to pander to the mob, chose not to incite a riot, and sidestepped the temptation to overpower the resident authority and claim an earthly throne, a kingdom locked into time and space. Instead he took his disciples aside for one last meal together, broke bread with them, and again dropped the bombshell that he was going to die. "You do not realize now what I am doing, but later you will understand" (John 13:7, NIV).

"Excuse me?" his friends must have said. "Would you run that by us again? We were just getting used to the servant stuff, and we really liked the whole Triumphal Entry thing. But now you say, 'This is my body, broken for you'? 'This is my blood—as often as you drink it'?"

"So listen already," Jesus must have said, "while I go over the highlights one more time."

THIS WILL BE OUR STUDY

And this will be our study during these next crucial weeks leading up to Easter, to go over the highlights one more time. We'll be using the Gospel of John, chapters 12–20 as our guide, but we'll sample some from the other narratives as we fill in a few more of the details.

Most importantly, we'll be doing it with Jesus, with all those original Jesus-followers, and with the last words Jesus offered—one more time—at the Last Supper.

Write the prayer below on a card and carry it with you today as a reminder of this commitment to learn and grow during this Lenten season.

Prayer: Bless us, Great Creator, with hearts open to hear your radical and compelling message. Teach us through these forty-plus days. Fill us with your Spirit. Guide us into a greater understanding of your radical love. Amen.

Day Five: Saturday

THE KEY WORD IS FORGIVENESS

Read John 13:18-30.

After saying this Jesus was troubled in spirit, and declared, "Very truly, I tell you, one of you will betray me" (v. 21).

I can imagine the scene: the casual glances around the room, the shifts in posture, the sideways looks, and the sense of affront elicited by a well-honed truth.

And I know that look, the one the disciples give Jesus when he calls them out. I used to teach middle school and, believe me, I know. It's the same look a thirteen-year-old boy will give when you stop him on his way to doing something inappropriate, and he simply can't fathom how in the universe his teacher can read his mind so clearly. So he employs the only strategy he knows—denial.

"Not me, Lord; no how, no way. . . ." I can see them, twelve guys nervously fidgeting in their seats, ready to finger one of their friends. Because they all know that they are capable, they all know that betrayal had already happened in so many ways, and they are all wondering if Jesus had really figured them out.

Well, they need not have worried. One of the great things about Jesus is that he does figure us out. That kind of realization takes the pressure off, really. There's comfort in the understanding that we can't fool God any more than we can fool ourselves.

Remember how the Teacher pointed out that the truth has the power to set each one of us free (John 8:32)? It's a principle that sets up the imperative for honesty and allows you—in fact requires you—to take things from there.

CONFESSION

Why do you think that confession forms such an important element in traditional worship? Because confession clears the air so well and gives us a chance to acknowledge on our own volition the truth that God already knows:

- Yes, I've messed up.
- Yes, I confess that I have and always will come up short of God's best.
- Yes, I know that I need forgiveness—and in so many ways.

I remember one particular life-changing New Year's resolution that I made one optimistic New Year's Day. It was nothing like "lose weight," "jog daily," or "use my credit card less," although I must admit each of those ideas has merit. No, this one was my best resolution ever. "I resolve to actively and deliberately try to *be the presence of Christ* in my work environment," I said. It proved to be one of the hardest and best decisions I have ever made.

Being the presence of Christ is a great concept for me, much better than handing out tracts on street corners or doing the whole "angry bullhorn" thing to strangers at the mall or on the street. The problem, however, is my constant failure, my inherent lack of spiritual depth rudely shoving its way through my resolve and into the forefront. That's when I fall short of being, as Paul puts it, "Christ's ambassador" (see 2 Cor. 5:20), and I really am betraying Jesus in much the way that he predicted.

COMPLICIT IN BETRAYAL?

Betrayal is a tough concept to consider, and we usually are more than happy to pin the rap on Judas. But remember, Peter also betrayed Jesus. The difference seems to be that Peter accepted forgiveness and then moved on whereas, tragically, Judas was unable to let Jesus love him that way. As for me, I tend to be more like Judas. I need to be open with Jesus and let him love me too.

When we confess our shortcomings, God is faithful and just to forgive us those things that stand between us and God. "If we say that we have no sin, we deceive ourselves, and the truth is not in us. If we confess our sins, he who is faithful and just will forgive us our sins and cleanse us from all unrighteousness. If we say that we have not sinned, we make him a liar, and his word is not in us" (1 John 1:8-10).

The key word in this passage is not betrayal; it's not even sin. The key word is *forgiveness*.

Re-read the questions on page 24. In what ways do you need forgiveness most today?

Prayer: We understand that we betray you every day, Jesus. Help us to walk more clearly in your light, and grant us peace as we walk in the truth of the forgiveness that you purchased at such enormous cost. Amen.

DEMOLITION AND RENOVATION

Read John 13:31-38.

The crowd answered him, "We have heard from the law that the Messiah remains forever. How can you say that the Son of Man must be lifted up? Who is this Son of Man?" Jesus said to them, "The light is with you for a little longer. Walk while you have the light, so that the darkness may not overtake you. If you walk in the darkness, you do not know where you are going. While you have the light, believe in the light, so that you may become children of light" (vv. 34-36).

The other morning Rebekah and I watched a home renovation show while sipping coffee and trying to ease slowly into what promised to be a very busy Saturday. The show focused on the disturbing fact that more often than we realize, contractors hired to do remodeling simply don't do the job properly. Not only is work sometimes botched or in violation of building codes, but some contractors also knowingly cover it up, take the money, and move on to another job. The home owners are left with problems they are not equipped to deal with and for which they often don't have the money to fix.

The one-hour show went on to document the problems that needed to be addressed, brought in a team of experts, pointed out what can be done differently and better, and then—my favorite part—the host literally intervened to rescue the home owners from the unfolding nightmare.

DEMOLITION!

Just about every intervention involves a period of extensive demolition. Floors are pulled up, walls torn down, ceilings removed, plumbing jack hammered out of the concrete and electrical wiring completely removed. One thing tends to lead to another until the full extent of the cover-up is exposed and the ultimate root of the problem can be corrected.

LENT TIE-IN

Today marks the first Sunday in the season of Lent. This is the time of preparation for the coming glory of Easter. But it occurs to me that I will never really be ready for anything that Christ offers until I'm first willing to look beneath the surface and deal with the shoddy workmanship—often cumulative over time—that too often characterizes the way I do business as a human being in the day in, day out living of my life.

Jesus did not come to work on my façade. Jesus lived and taught and suffered and addressed death head-on in order to set me free. Freedom goes a lot deeper than appearance.

The scripture for today talks about light. Simply put, we need light to see clearly or nothing really changes. Christ offers such light, providing a view of our need that is incisive, penetrating, and unconstrained by the niceties of social posturing. The light Jesus applies brings healing along with revelation. Instead of condemnation, Jesus offers liberation and love.

Earlier in John's story of the good news, Jesus made his purpose clear: "Indeed, God did not send the Son into the world to condemn the world, but in order that the world might be saved through him" (John 3:17). This weekend, if you're reading along with any sense of seriously engaging this journey through Lent, why not ask Jesus to bring light to your dark places? And then have the courage to embark on some meaningful renovation work.

As the guy on the TV show likes to say, "Let's make this right!"

Prayer: Sometimes fear comes in along with talk of renovation. God, Light of the universe, please bring assurance with your evaluation. Grant us courage, and the wisdom to get on with the work that needs to be done. Amen.

I WISH I COULD HAVE BEEN THERE

Read John 14:1-8.

> *Thomas said to him, "Lord, we do not know where you are going. How can we know the way?" (v. 5).*

Back in the early 1980s I read a little book titled *If You Don't Know Where You're Going, You'll Probably End Up Somewhere Else*. The central idea was not far removed from that of books like *The Purpose Driven Life*, or *The 7 Habits of Highly Effective People*. Too many of us live without any clear sense of vision and, as the Bible points out, "Where there is no vision, the people perish" (Prov. 29:18, KJV).

So Jesus talked with his friends, going over the highlights one more time, telling them about the place he is preparing for their future. And Thomas, never one to hold back his true feelings or his doubts, asks the obvious question: "We don't have any idea where you're going, so how can we know the way?" (author's paraphrase).

Jesus must have paused in the moment, maybe raised an eyebrow or inclined his head, and reflected on all that he had said, all that he had taught during the years that he had lived with these men and women. And I can envision him leaning back and smiling knowingly, opening his hands expansively to take in every single soul in that room. They must have sensed it too, capturing the moment with rapt attention, leaning in as one body to hear the Jesus' response to the question Thomas had posed.

"I am the way, and the truth, and the life," Jesus says, his eyes overflowing with love and compassion. "No one comes to the Father except through me" (John 14:6).

I can see Jesus pausing, making eye contact with each of his friends in the room, and deliberately and lovingly drawing them into his spirit. "If you really know me," he continues, willing them to know him, "you would know my Father as well. From now on," and here he too leans forward into the tightening circle, "you do know him and have seen him" (v. 7, author's paraphrase).

I imagine that you could have heard a pin drop. It was one of those defining moments, an experience from which you emerge with more clarity than you ever imagined.

I WISH I COULD HAVE BEEN THERE

I wish I could have been there, sitting at the table, leaning in toward Jesus, hanging on to the words of life. There are many scenes from the Gospels that I am drawn to. But this one, where Jesus dropped such an incredible truth right into the disciples' laps, would have been special.

Of course, such illuminating moments are always a possibility, even today, because the ministry of Jesus is not merely historical, it is current, right here in the middle of real life. How would we choose to respond to such an opportunity today? What would we have our best friend and teacher share with us, right now, at this moment? How much of the truth are we prepared to hear now, where we are, on our knees?

This would be a good moment to talk with Jesus about it, one on one.

Prayer: It is hard to kneel. Yet we do: contrite, submissive, and eager to learn. Teach us, heal us, and love us, we pray. Amen.

THE JESUS IMPERATIVE

Read John 14:9-14.

> *"How can you say, 'Show us the Father'? Do you not believe that I am in the*
> *Father and the Father is in me? The words that I say to you I do not speak*
> *on my own; but the Father who dwells in me does his works. Believe me that*
> *I am in the Father and the Father is in me" (vv. 9-11).*

I love the language the great Teacher uses here, always schooling his listeners about the nature of God. Jesus is the interface of time and eternity, the known and the unknown, spirit and matter, the natural and the supernatural.

This is Incarnation, another moment when God, in Jesus, breaks quite literally into time and space. We have no adequate language for God—no way to conceptualize eternity, perfection, completeness, omniscience, or holiness. The Jews were on to something when they did not speak God's name as a sign of reverence. But Jesus called the Father "Abba," Daddy. And then he said that we too could know God in the same way.

We see in today's reading that God's intentions were focused into this flesh-and-blood world through the lens of Jesus. We see also that the Creator intends that kind of work to continue through all of us privileged to call ourselves Jesus' followers.

BELIEF

Our foundational beliefs, Jesus suggests, are a critical factor in determining how we think, speak, and ultimately act. In other words, what we believe profoundly affects the manner in which we live. I think that Jesus understood this better than anyone else in history.

Jesus invites us to participate in the God-life in much the same way that he does. I honestly don't think that Jesus came into this world preloaded with infinite knowledge and superhero abilities—kind of a GOD-version 7.7. Instead, it's my opinion that Jesus had the opportunity and the responsibility to live and learn and grow and develop with the same reality-based constraints we all have to contend with. The difference is that Jesus, God made flesh, not only "increased in wisdom and stature" (Luke 2:52, NIV) but also surpassed all human expectations.

Jesus brought to the table the clarity of his belief. Jesus knew that he was in the Father and the Father was in him, and he understood how dramatically and conclusively belief affects everything else. That's why he was constantly raising the question, and he parsed it again in the scripture we're looking at today. Jesus challenged his friends to believe that God literally inhabited him, and that God "does his works" (v. 10) in and through the life he was living among his friends.

SALVATION

One of the most helpful definitions of salvation that I've come across can be expressed as "participating in the work of God." Jesus challenged the disciples to believe, so that they too could participate in the good work that God is up to in the world.

So in the last few days before he was killed by the people his radical ideas threaten, Jesus lays out what is important. He tries to make his friends understand that they will not "see the Father" in the traditional ways that they are used to imagining God, or via the ways they think they need to experience God. God, Jesus points out, is best understood and experienced in terms of allowing God's work to take up residence in us, and then to believe, and, consequently, to live.

THE JESUS IMPERATIVE

"Live!" That's the Jesus imperative. And it's a good word to conclude the first full week of Lent.

"Take the trouble to know me," Jesus continues the thought from the question Thomas had posed earlier. "Take the trouble to know me and you will also know the Father. If you know God's will, and then pray accordingly, greater things still are going to happen because you dare the commitment" (John 14:10-11, author paraphrase).

Prayer: Use me, Lord, use even me. Take me; melt me; break me; mold me; fill me. Amen.

"IF YOU SAY THAT YOU LOVE ME"

Read John 14:15-17.

"If you love me, you will keep my commandments. And I will ask the Father, and he will give you another Advocate, to be with you forever" (vv. 15-16).

Today I'm caught up in the memory of my cousin Linda. She died this past week, just forty-six years of age. But she demonstrated such wondrous grace and faith as she realized that the life she knew, in this time and space, was coming to a close.

Linda was an arrestingly lovely lady, both beautiful and spiritually astute. She owned a vibrant sense of life and the kind of "live-it-out-loud" application of faith that engages the deepest meaning of Lent's redemptive focus. Linda lived the powerful truth that, because of Jesus' passion and resurrection, the reality of eternity is held in every moment: life, death, and, sometimes most poignantly, the transition between the two.

I sensed all of this acutely during a wonderful conversation I had with Linda and her husband, Dave, via Skype the first week of December. We talked for close to an hour. Then, at the end of the conversation, we prayed together. I wish we all could have taken one another's hands. But it was interesting how prayer linked us inexplicably, and I could barely speak through the tears. It was as if a different kind of conduit had opened up the moment we began to pray.

So there is communication, and then there is *communication*. The content of the entire conversation was necessarily deep, but something else happened when faith entered the equation. "Perfect love," John said, "drives out fear"

(1 John 4:18, NIV). And, as Jesus promised, "But take heart! I have overcome [conquered] the world" (John 16:33, NIV).

I wrote the following entry in my blog the day after that conversation:

I've said before that my cousin Linda is a cool lady, full of grace and strength. Well, she'd say it isn't her, that the grace is all God—and even more the strength part. But that is what happens when you don't really know anymore where you come to an end and where God begins.

I'm thankful that, as who Linda is becomes more and more defined by eternity than it is by time, my cousin's faith is something that we all can embrace, and that God's powerful presence is all about the fullness of life. I pray that we all might know the assurance of such faith and love.

JESUS-FOLLOWER

Question: What are some of the biggest stumbling blocks that keep nonbelievers from darkening the doors of their local Christian church?

Answer: A lack of authenticity, church politics, and the hard-to-hide truth that the real-deal, Jesus kind of love is seldom central to community life.

I guess that I'm saying my cousin Linda was a bona fide Jesus follower. Jesus was crystal clear regarding what he wanted to see when it came to that kind of label. And it's safe to say that the Lord wasn't looking for correct doctrine or outward appearances or a social political slant.

"If you love me," Jesus said, "you will keep my commandments" (John 14:15). Such a simple admonition. Jesus shows us the way, plain and simple. "All right then. I'll use small words and speak slowly. Listen up: if you love me—if you truly say that you love me, then follow my directions; demonstrate my love; keep my commandments."

"Oh, but Lord," we all want to say, "you mentioned something about loving the Lord God with all our heart, all our strength, all our mind, all our soul, and loving our neighbor as ourselves. Isn't that too broad a concept? I mean, what is love anyway?"

Jesus: "No one has greater love than this, to lay down one's life for one's friends" (John 15:13).

Us: "OK, Lord, we don't have to go there. But my mind? Get serious! Our minds are so complex that psychologists are still trying to figure out the basics."

Jesus: "Be transformed by the renewing of your minds" (Rom. 12:2).

Us: "That's not fair, Lord. Paul said that much later. Oh, never mind. Listen, Lord, our lives are very complicated. How can we possibly keep all of your commandments? I mean, isn't that just a tad unreasonable? Can't we be selective? You really are a little too radical for us sometimes."

Jesus: "If you keep my commandments, you will abide in my love" (John 15:10).

When we follow Jesus, the Christ-life becomes our life and, like my cousin Linda, the application by definition is systemic and never merely topical.

So where is the place that you end and God begins? It turns out that there is no such place for those who follow closely. Contemplate the implications of that truth in your life.

Prayer: Challenge us gently, Lord. Show us the way. And grant us courage. Amen.

Day Ten: Thursday

PROMISE TRANSLATED INTO LOVE

Read John 14:15-21.

> *"I will ask the Father, and he will give you another Advocate, to be with you forever. This is the Spirit of truth, whom the world cannot receive, because it neither sees him nor knows him. You know him, because he abides with you, and he will be in you.*
>
> *I will not leave you orphaned; I am coming to you. In a little while the world will no longer see me, but you will see me; because I live, you also will live. On that day you will know that I am in my Father, and you in me, and I in you"* (vv. 16-20).

Eternity has been an emerging theme in my thinking about Lent, which is not surprising, considering that Jesus' mission consisted in large part of erasing the lines of distinction between this world and the kingdom of God. But death remains a persistent fact of life. The reality of the death of loved ones is often difficult for us, but at the same time the experience can speak to the mystery of eternity with comforting clarity.

The story I recounted yesterday about my cousin reminded me of the summer I just missed saying good-bye to my grandfather Fred. We knew he was ailing, and all the Mauls (including our son, Andrew, just fourteen months at the time) were heading to England for a rare, four-generation photo. Instead, we made it just in time to attend the memorial service.

I remember sitting in Grandpa's study with my Aunt Gladys. We were all missing him profoundly and trying to connect with his memory. She took a book from his desktop and opened it up. It was his Bible. I noticed that instead of replacing the worn scriptures, my grandfather had had his Bible rebound, perhaps several times over the years. Consequently, all of his carefully written notes and annotations were preserved, from the day in the early 1920s that he first opened its pages through over sixty years of faith, family, business, and struggle.

Inside the front cover my aunt found a series of important dates—birth, death, declarations of war, celebrations of peace—and my grandfather's prayers and observations. And there, in my grandfather's distinctive handwriting, she found the record of her own birth: "Born today, a beautiful baby girl; we shall call her Gladys. Dear Gladys, one day you will read this. . . ." Following were more words of hope, encouragement, consolation, and peace.

TIME BEYOND TIME

We caught my grandfather's spirit that afternoon. Warm, tangible, timely. Through his words we all felt a significant measure of his love and intention; the effect was real.

Jesus promises us so much more than the run of the mill or the mundane. He promises the comfort of the Holy Spirit, God with us in every small detail of our lives. There is no magic to this concept, simply the promise of Jesus translated into love.

"God will abide in you," Jesus assured his friends. "God will take up residence within the very essence of who you are. This is my gift; this is my power; this is my comfort. Through the gift of the Holy Spirit, you will know completely that I am alive and that I am vitally involved in your every moment. I love you. Be comforted" (John 14:17-20, author paraphrase).

That promise is often translated into love through the people God brings into our lives. When and how have you felt the working of the Holy Spirit in your life?

Prayer: May the beauty of your holiness rest in each one of us; may the assurance of your love comfort us; may the active presence of your Spirit take up residence in our consciousness. Amen.

Day Eleven: Friday

LIVING AS IF WE MEAN IT—BECAUSE GOD MOST CERTAINLY DOES

Read John 14:18-24.

> *"I will not leave you orphaned; I am coming to you. In a little while the world will no longer see me, but you will see me; because I live, you also will live" (vv. 18-19).*

IRREPRESSIBLE LIFE

Apart from the agenda on my daily calendar—"write column, pack for tomorrow's flight, complete prep for teaching at retreat, run off message for Sunday morning, line up interviews for next week"—I make no predictions about what will happen over the next twenty-four hours or so. There are too many variables interfacing everything I intend to do and any number of things can and most certainly will happen to confound my plans.

But Jesus knew exactly what was coming at him. He knew it as he talked with his friends around the table in the upper room, and I believe it contributed to the urgency of his words. The immediate future was alarmingly clear, and Jesus revealed tremendous strength and honest bravery as he understood the inevitability of betrayal, torture, and death.

In complete humanity, both at odds with and beautifully complementary to his uncompromised deity, Jesus moved toward all the horror that the ensuing day and a half had in store.

In today's scripture selection from John's account of the Last Supper, Jesus speaks plainly and eloquently about the mystery that defines God's grace, as he draws logical conclusions regarding our relationship to God based on his relationship with us.

I remember the way I was received into my wife's family. Rebekah's mother loved me instantly and without reserve both because she loved Rebekah and Rebekah loves me and also because I make Rebekah happy. It's a lot like that with God. We love Jesus; Jesus loved us enough to die for us; God loves the Son; and we are all adopted into this family by virtue of Jesus' great love for us. God the Father accepts and cherishes me—Derek Maul—not on my merit, but because Jesus died for me, loves me, and presents me just as I am at God's Communion Table, as his very own brother. (See Rom. 5:8.)

Not only that, but Jesus points out how I will come to receive this fullness of life. It's the same principle that applies to each one of us. "It's the life that I experience," Jesus explained in many ways over the course of the evening, and that life will be ours in equal measure. Then, conclusively, "Because I live, you also will live" (v. 19).

FAMILY

Our status as the brothers and the sisters of Jesus means that we share in that same life: the Christ-vitality, the deep and larger-than-life aliveness. The world around us, broken and cynical, may not see Jesus. The world may believe that Christ is defeated and defunct; but we know that the Christ-life is alive and vibrant and real.

Then, and here's the kicker, the world—this ambient culture where we hang out in the everyday grind—gets the opportunity to see firsthand the compelling evidence of the resurrection in us. Because we, the church, are advertised throughout the New Testament as "the body of Christ." What changes can you make in your life that will make that clear to others?

Prayer: Please live in us and through us, Jesus. Let us live more completely in the truth of your message. Amen.

GOD-SATURATED BEHAVIOR

Read John 14:25-27.

"Peace I leave with you; my peace I give to you. I do not give to you as the world gives. Do not let your hearts be troubled, and do not let them be afraid" (v. 27).

Do not remember the former things,
or consider the things of old.
I am about to do a new thing;
now it springs forth, do you not perceive it?
I will make a way in the wilderness
and rivers in the desert. (Isaiah 43:18-19)

When people ran into Jesus they often had good reason to remember the encounter. Sometimes he infuriated them; sometimes he made perfect sense; and sometimes he did both. Regardless, those who encountered Jesus often left challenged, knowing the possibility of the kind of peace that the world had never offered before.

Jesus' style of peace entails not simply resting in the presence of God so much as moving forward in the presence of God. Peace requires God-saturated behavior. Peace refers to a state of being more than a state of mind. Peace is an action word. That's why Jesus said, "I do not give to you as the world gives." Jesus settles the troubled heart, sometimes by troubling the settled life.

DATELINE FOLKESTONE, ENGLAND

During a recent trip to England I made a visit to my hometown, where I was born and lived the first nineteen years of my life. Folkestone is on the southern coast of England, a few miles west of Dover in the county of Kent. It's on the Straits of Dover, as close to France as England gets.

I had just a few hours, so I looked at the breathtaking scenery from the hills, walked around my old neighborhood, and then parked in the town center so I could explore some more. I discovered a new "superstore" downtown, with its own multistory parking garage. The roof offered me a view, looking east toward Dover, that I had never seen before. I thought I knew what the town looked like, but it turns out there is always a new perspective, a fresh orientation, and a more innovative view.

WHAT IF?

And so I walked around my old hometown with new eyes, seeing it as if for the very first time, not only with the perspective of a grown man but also with the vision of someone who hadn't lived there for thirty-four years. I owned a new perspective because I'd never before looked at the town from that particular vantage point, a hundred or so feet above the city center.

This is exactly what I'd like to see us do with Easter. I'd like to see us standing in a new place, somewhere outside the realm of the familiar, taking a look at Jesus' cross, passion, and resurrection—beholding with new eyes!

Imagine arriving at Palm Sunday (the week before Easter) with your devotional life finely tuned, your daily understanding of God's grace well-practiced, your walk with Jesus in full stride, and your sense of expectation fully engaged. Consider the implications:

- What if we allowed everything that Jesus achieved and is achieving to impact us as if we had heard it for the very first time?
- What if we've been looking at forty days of Lent from the standpoint of tradition rather than living faith?
- What if our understanding of Easter has everything to do with religion and almost nothing to do with a transformational encounter with the living God?
- What if we did something new this year, and all of that changed?

I don't know what the result would be, I'm just asking the questions. But then again, I'm asking because I already know from personal experience what can happen when someone stands in a new place and asks new questions.

How about you?

Prayer: We all have something to do today that has the potential to be exclusively kingdom-oriented behavior. Guide us in these few quiet moments to listen to your voice, God, and to bring your kind of peace into this anxiety-ridden world. Amen.

Day Thirteen: The Second Sunday in Lent
THE PRINCE OF THIS WORLD

Read John 14:25-31.

"I will not speak with you much longer, for the prince of this world is coming. He has no hold on me, but the world must learn that I love the Father and that I do exactly what my Father has commanded me" (vv. 30-31, NIV).

If you are ever tempted to doubt the reality of evil as an active force in this world, simply remember that Jesus believed it to be so. A single-dimensional outlook, unwilling to confront the possibility of darkness simply plays into the hands of evil. In C. S. Lewis's classic book *The Screwtape Letters*, the crafty older demon acknowledges that the cause of evil accrues much more power when Christians fail to concede that it exists.

At the same time we also have to understand that, as children of light, evil has no long-term power over us. But it's not that easy to defeat an enemy if we refuse to name it. Having named evil for what it is, we can go on to declare that "at the name of Jesus every knee shall bend in heaven and on earth and under the earth, and every tongue confess that Jesus Christ is Lord" (Phil. 2:10-11). Darkness has no hold on Christ or on followers of the Way.

Evil may have no power over us, but this assurance comes with the condition that we commit to follow the Jesus Way. Which is why Jesus often talked about the importance of following the laws and commandments of God.

Why do we refuse to name the evil as evil? We've all heard people dismiss any talk of proactive evil as narrow and old-fashioned thinking, as superstitious nonsense, as just another form of legalism, or as echoes of the unenlightened past. Or we may just want to avoid an unpleasant subject. I don't like it so we won't talk about it! Besides, doesn't all this talk about following

God's laws smack of legalism? Wouldn't strictly following rules make us like robots, afraid to step off the straight and narrow?

The problem is not legalism so much as proximity. Following God's commandments does not make us robots. It simply makes sense to follow God's instructions because we love God. But when we stray from the path of obedience it's typically because we've drifted away from God and our relationship to the source of light has broken down, not because we have forgotten some trivial rule. "Where the Spirit of the Lord is," the Bible tells us, "there is liberty" (2 Cor. 3:17, KJV).

Proximity control is a useful practice for Lent. If we seriously want to remain on "the straight and narrow path," then why not make the effort to place ourselves where we know we will meet Jesus on a regular basis? If we do, then it stands to reason we'll know the way. This commitment makes the way of the Cross our very own and invites light and life as our constant companion. That's when the pilgrim path becomes increasingly natural and clear.

Christ's assurance gives both hope and freedom. What a remarkable place to be! What a clearly defined opportunity for a life that makes sense. What a wonderful and gracious God to show us the way.

Prayer: Thank you so much, gracious God, for assurance and hope and freedom. It is our sure knowledge of your love and our experience of your forgiveness that makes us free; free to follow you and free to give ourselves away because we love you so much. Amen.

I DON'T THINK WE'RE IN KANSAS ANYMORE

Read John 15:1-8.

> *"Abide in me as I abide in you. Just as the branch cannot bear fruit by itself unless it abides in the vine, neither can you unless you abide in me" (v. 4).*

My wife and I often read together at the end of the day. We both typically have a couple of books going at any given time. Occasionally we'll try to read something considered "classic," either in response to a recommendation or because we've consumed one too many mysteries and feel the need to digest some good literature and continue our education. Consequently, Rebekah was wrestling with some fifteenth-century philosophy recently, and the experience was nothing short of painful. She read a section aloud, and I agreed it probably wasn't worth the effort.

"The thinking is five hundred years old," she said. "I guess thought has changed so much that it's not surprising it doesn't ring true anymore."

"But wait," I countered. "Jesus' words in the New Testament were written two thousand years ago. They haven't lost any of their impact."

This passage from John 15 is a great example: "Abide in me as I abide in you. Just as the branch cannot bear fruit by itself unless it abides in the vine, neither can you unless you abide in me." Another translation offers "remain" in place of "abide." Christ's words resonate through time; they ring true regardless of the phrasing.

I DON'T THINK WE'RE IN KANSAS ANY MORE

A couple of years ago I was invited to speak at a "Men's Charge" event (they weren't interested, they said, in retreating) in a small-town in Kansas. Men from several churches gathered together for fellowship, discussion, learning, and mutual encouragement.

These guys were living Jesus truth out loud, the spiritual truth that Jesus articulated when he said "No branch can bear fruit by itself" (v. 4, NIV). The leaders came from three local congregations: the Baptist Church, the Church of Christ, and the United Methodist Church. In this particular community, the enthusiastic participation of those three churches in an "I am the vine, you are the vine, we are the vine together" event was explained to me as nothing short of a major miracle.

I imagine Jesus' reaction being, "No duh! My body is a connectional system. You need me; and because of the way the Father designed things, you also need one another. To abide in me, to 'remain' in me, you've gotta stay connected to the vine; end of story."

WISTERIA

When we lived in Pensacola we had a troublesome wisteria vine that would never stop cropping up all over. One of its favorite venues was the telephone pole on the edge of our property; it also liked the adjacent fence. The thing was relentless.

Every once in a while I'd go out with huge pruning shears and cut the creeper carefully where it first emerged from the ground. In a few hours, fifty-plus feet of wisteria would droop, then turn brown. A few days later I could easily pull it all down.

Jesus wants us to understand that we are as vitally connected to him and to one another, as that wisteria is to its source of life. Without sustaining grace we simply wither and die.

The local faith community is part of the system of sustenance that keeps each one of us connected and nourished. When I say "the community of faith," I don't mean my denomination or yours. The church—any church—is supposed to be recognized as "the body of Christ" because Jesus reaches out to the world through followers of the Way. It's through us that the vine continues to grow and bear fruit.

Growth is a vital part of a meaningful life; Jesus was unequivocal regarding this principle. And life in Christ is never stagnant, quiescent, or listless. Rot and decay have no place in the vine. "The fruit of the Spirit is love, joy, peace, patience, kindness, generosity, faithfulness, gentleness, and self-control. There is no law against such things" (Gal. 5:22-23).

"Check out the fruit," Jesus said on more than one occasion. "That's how you're going to know my disciples" (see Matt. 7:16). "If we love one another, God lives in us, and his love is perfected in us" (1 John 4:12).

What fruit do you offer?

Prayer: Help us to recognize our deep thirst, God. Then fill us with your grace. Amen.

Day Fifteen: Tuesday

FRIENDS OF GOD

Read John 15:9-17.

> *"I do not call you servants any longer, because the servant does not know what the master is doing; but I have called you friends, because I have made known to you everything that I have heard from my Father" (v. 15).*

Sometimes I try to get my mind around the astonishing fact that Jesus values me—Derek Maul—as a friend. Christ Jesus—the Son of the living God, begotten not created, of one substance (*homoousia*) with the Father, Emmanuel, Creator of the Universe, Prince of Peace—has made the deliberate point of calling me friend.

Typically, I don't stop to think about just how mind-boggling this is. But the truth of this is huge, so much so that absolutely nothing can compare.

To put the idea into perspective, think about those people you know who are name-droppers (maybe you're one yourself). "Yes, senator so and so. . . ." "She's a neighbor of mine. . . ." "Played golf with her husband. . . ." "They always send us a Christmas card. . . ." "Cute kids. . . ." "I'm on her speed dial. . . ."

FRIENDS WITH THE QUEEN OF ENGLAND

In the English world of who-knows-whom, a series of ever-wider circles emanates from the social epicenter known as "the Royal Family" (or "the Royals," for those in the know). Jockeying for position and trying to be in contact with persons one level closer to "the Royals" is serious business for social climbers. People achieve something resembling Nirvana when Queen Elizabeth II actually calls them by name. (I know this because my second cousin on my mother's side is one of the Queen's close friends. He saved her life once, and she likes to play Monopoly with him.)

Seriously, though, my cousin's relationship to the Queen of England really doesn't matter; it has no bearing on my life. What does matter is my relationship to God, and it's stunning when we think about what that means. The King of kings and Lord of lords knows us by name. God calls us "friend." Can we grasp even a small part of what that really means? I'm not sure that I can.

"And I love you so much," Jesus said, "that I went to the lengths of laying down my life for you. Do you understand the measure of how much you mean to me? Peter, Thomas, Mary, Judas, David, Gerard, Sally, Derek, Steve, Robin, Gary, Rebekah, JoEllen, Darrell, Kirk, Karin, Charles, Lee?"

BEYOND SOCIAL NETWORKING

To put the idea into modern terms, as a friend said in a recent message, "Jesus wants to be your friend on Facebook."

Jesus loves so unreservedly that the concepts of obedience, affection, joy, and death can all be uttered in the same paragraph. Remember the fruit of the vine we were talking about yesterday? That fruit is love. It is deeply personal; it comes from the highest levels; and it is alive.

Prayer: You walked right into the garden of Gethsemane knowing everything, Jesus. You knew exactly what would happen, and you valued our relationship more than your own life. I'm so glad that I do not need to earn such friendship in terms of my status or my achievements. I can't imagine where I would be if you held strictly to the requirements of the law. Instead, you call me friend. Thank you for your gracious acceptance and your honest love. Amen.

LIVING IN THE TRUTH

Read John 15:18-27.

> *"When the Advocate comes, whom I will send to you from the Father, the Spirit of truth who comes from the Father, he will testify on my behalf. You also are to testify because you have been with me from the beginning"* *(vv. 26-27).*

In Acts 4, Peter and John model what it is to testify truly. Their method did not entail yelling at the crowds, forcing tracts on them, or telling them that they were bound directly for hell if they didn't believe just like them. When ordered by the authorities to keep quiet about Jesus, they simply appealed to the standard generally applied to witnesses in court, to tell the truth about what they had seen. "We cannot keep from speaking about what we have seen and heard" (v. 20). The two friends were eyewitness to what they knew; nothing more and nothing less.

I always think about Peter and John's example when I have the opportunity to talk with a new acquaintance. It's what happened when I was "flying the friendly skies" again recently. I sat next to a lawyer and former state attorney general; the man was a bona fide character. He noticed I was reading from my first book, *Get Real: A Spiritual Journey for Men.* We talked about faith for a while.

"My wife is really interested in that kind of thing" was all he was willing to say.

He told me that he was returning from a mission to hand deliver a check for $260,000 to a struggling family in South Florida. It was the last action of a complex trust settlement and the recipients had no idea that they were beneficiaries. They didn't know what was coming.

"Did they accept the check?" I asked.

"Of course," he replied.

"Were you enthusiastic about delivering the money?" I asked. "Or did you just hand over the check and walk away?"

"Are you kidding? It was a great experience!" he said. "Why do you ask?"

I was thinking about faith again. We have this amazing gift, this trust, a treasure much more remarkable than two hundred sixty thousand dollars. We can't begin to put a monetary value on a relationship with the living God. Our job is to deliver the news of that relationship to others. Yet, more often than not, we fail to deliver the news with any real enthusiasm, and people decline the inheritance as if they're merely passing up another magazine subscription or a life insurance sales pitch.

I've been wearing out one particular theme recently; it's foundational to everything I share. But the idea bears repeating because the implications are so powerful and far-reaching: "We need to live as if we mean it! Why? Because God most certainly does."

I'm convinced that if more people of faith lived in a spirit of authentic meaning, modeling a vital comprehension of the implications of grace, an understanding that helps us focus on our very foundations as people, then it wouldn't be so hard, or so false, or so staged for us to share the good news. Instead, we'd simply—and profoundly—live in a manner that reveals the truth.

What changes in your life would help you accomplish that goal?

Prayer: We have this great treasure, God, and we so often treat it as if it's nothing all that important. How could we have forgotten the cost? How can we be so cavalier about the gift of meaning? How can we help but talk about what we have seen and heard? Amen.

Day Seventeen: Thursday

DESIGNED FOR SUPPORTIVE COMMUNITY

Read John 16:1-4.

"I have said these things to you to keep you from stumbling" (v. 1).

Recently my "Men's-Room" Bible study group at church changed its typical routine. Several of my "most excellent dudes" are involved in ongoing hunger ministry programs, and we wanted to raise both awareness and dollars for our congregation's feeding initiatives. At the same time, we hoped to recruit some additional men to join our ongoing Bible study. So we invited a handful of potential members to join us for a dinner, and we challenged ourselves to step out of the box.

The night of the meeting, after we gathered indoors and said the blessing, I led the group outside to the church parking lot. There my friend Gerard opened his trunk and handed each person a brown-paper bag, packed with a simple sandwich and fruit and a bottle of water. In other words, we handled the meal no differently than the outreach to homeless folk that takes place in the various places they hang out around our town. We then shared a powerful time around folding tables, talking about the deep impact that hunger ministries have on those privileged to participate.

THE CALL TO DISCIPLESHIP

The call to be disciples, to live faith out loud in response to our deliberate and purposeful decision to follow Jesus, necessarily includes acts of mercy and kindness. In fact, the more time we spend in the presence of Christ, the more our fundamental lifestyle can't help but incorporate Christlikeness. Then, as we listen more attentively to God's voice, specific acts of mercy and kindness will give way to lives functionally defined by those qualities. Instead of an occasional, "as needed" application of religion, the nature of Jesus becomes a new and living way.

Most of the Bible verses we're referencing during these forty days of Lent (plus six Sundays) come from John's account of the Last Supper. Jesus seems concerned that his friends still don't quite understand the full import of what he is saying. "All this I have told you so that you will not go astray," Jesus points out (John 16:1, NIV). It's as if the Lord wants to hammer home the fundamentals of some of his essential teachings one last time.

LIVING IN COMMUNITY

That's one reason I am so committed to my Wednesday evening men's Bible study. God works powerfully and compellingly through the support and love of my brothers. This group of men is unafraid to hold one another accountable (although some of them still are a teensy-bit resistant to transparency beyond a certain threshold), and they all understand the value of prayer support and the power of ongoing backup during the week.

The time is best described as "my Wednesday grounding," and the hunger-action dinner that we held that night served as another one of those occasions that illustrated exactly how important we are to one another.

Pray seriously this week about being more deliberate when it comes to engaging the friendship of other believers, the people who demonstrate their love for God in the way that they love you. Then you can love them back, grow in faith, and together serve God more faithfully in—and for—this hurting world.

Prayer: You have gone to great lengths, caring God, to be present in our lives and to keep us from stumbling. Be with us as we consider your call to be more deliberately involved with other believers, to look for support as we grow in our faith, and to live as a real community of faithful followers of the Way. Amen.

Day Eighteen: Friday
JESUS GETS SERIOUS

Read John 16:1-7.

"They will put you out of the synagogues. Indeed, an hour is coming when those who kill you will think that by doing so they are offering worship to God. And they will do this because they have not known the Father or me" (vv. 2-3).

In 1975 I took a trip into the Soviet Union with a bus load of thirty-seven enthusiastic Christians. Apart from sightseeing and learning about the Eastern Bloc at the height of the Cold War, one of our goals was to deliver Bibles, encouragement, and much needed medical supplies to members of the underground church in the Ukraine.

My primary duty for the tour was to pack and unpack the decrepit truck that carried all the camping equipment, food, suitcases, and supplies we needed to support a bus load of people during three months of camping throughout Europe and the Middle East. Consequently, it fell to me to "assist" the intimidating set of officials who inspected our vehicles when we crossed the border from Romania into the USSR. Already deep behind the Iron Curtain, our moods darkened as we handed over our passports. The rude, bullying behavior of the guards only aggravated our sense of anxiety. They went so far during their inspection as to cut open our twenty-pound bags of rice and to empty our large containers of freeze-dried foods, making as big a mess as possible.

"We know you are Christian, yes?" a uniformed officer said to me from behind reflective sunglasses, his automatic weapon slung carelessly over one shoulder. "We guess you visit other Jesus people we do not know. Maybe you have letters, names, address? Very interesting for us."

INTIMIDATION

In addition to everything else in the truck, our leader had given me charge of three "special" suitcases stuffed full of medicine and Russian-language Bibles. I was nineteen years old and fearless (some would say reckless), so I carefully arranged an elaborate version of a "shell game" with all of our suitcases. The three that contained contraband were caught in an endless loop of passing, dumping, searching, and repacking. Mercifully, we made it through customs after nearly four grueling hours.

Our tour guide, "Nikita," spoke cryptically yet candidly with us as we gathered around the campfire that night. "Here in Soviet Union, we have no problems with secret police; what KGB boys do is *no* secret! We have other joke: KGB stand for 'Kind Good Boys.' Remember this, please, and be extra careful."

Pray specifically for Christians facing persecution. Share the challenge with your friends.

(Story to be continued.)

Prayer: Help us to understand, God of liberty, the tremendous blessings of our freedom here at home. Please be with those in other nations who are struggling with persecution and oppression, even as we pray. Amen.

BEHIND THE IRON CURTAIN WITH MUCH TO LEARN

Read John 16:7-15.

> *"When [the Advocate] comes, he will prove the world wrong about sin and righteousness and judgment: about sin, because they do not believe in me; about righteousness, because I am going to the Father and you will see me no longer; about judgment, because the ruler of this world has been condemned. I still have many things to say to you, but you cannot bear them now" (vv. 8-12).*

When our caravan arrived in Kiev in 1975, we immediately visited the official, registered Baptist church. The pastor there had made arrangements for us to pass our smuggled goods on to his colleague in the underground church. The pastor explained to me that being part of an officially registered congregation enabled the members to maintain access to basic services and minimal educational opportunities. In exchange for those benefits, however, Sunday school classes for children were prohibited; the content of his sermons was carefully reviewed by the state; and all church activities had to be preapproved, monitored, and corrected when unsatisfactory.

Participants in unregistered (and thus unmonitored) churches, on the other hand, suffered severe persecution if discovered. Their families were denied access to medical services; they were ineligible for advancement or careers other than menial employment; and educational opportunities were routinely withdrawn. Constant harassment, disappearances, sentences to the Gulag, and mysterious deaths (especially among the clergy) were common. Either way, the pastor explained, whether one was part of an officially registered congregation or an underground church, being identified as a Christian carried social and political costs.

Having learned this reality, with the romanticism and mystique of spy movies and novels now thoroughly behind me, I quickly unburdened myself of the three suitcases. I had obviously involved myself in a dangerous game, and it wasn't until we reached Yugoslavia almost two weeks later that my heart rate returned somewhere close to normal.

That was 1975, and it was an interesting trip in many regards (see *The Unmaking of a Part-time Christian*, Upper Room Books, 2009). On the other hand, being identified as a Christian has never been unduly troublesome here in the United States. I sometimes wonder, though, if my comfort results from my tendency to reinterpret Jesus' radical message so that it fits more easily into the affluent, consumer-driven society I enjoy. In consequence, the way I follow Jesus neither marks me as countercultural nor distinguishes me from others, so most people simply ignore me and leave me alone.

Philip Yancey, in his book *The Jesus I Never Knew*, suggests that we have recreated Jesus in a carefully crafted image, a rendition less threatening to standard modern day religious practice. Jesus has been sanitized, the rough edges sanded down, the radical fringe elements carefully rephrased, and repackaged so as not to offend.

That's not the reality that many Christians inhabit. Countless Christ followers all around the world are still being tortured and slaughtered because they dare to take seriously the radical message of their revolutionary Savior. Can we not at the very least take a more effective stand for goodness? A more costly position regarding justice? And be more self-sacrificial advocates for the kind of agenda that led Jesus to the Cross?

We can work to stop human trafficking, challenge racist conversation, thank God for food in public places, intentionally and openly practice the sabbath to keep it holy, and generally share the gospel by living lives directed by values rooted in Matthew 22:37-40: "Love God with the entirety of your being, and love your neighbor as yourself" (author paraphrase).

Our call is still to be countercultural. How will people know God, and how will anyone ever meet Jesus unless we are willing to put our security and ourselves on the line?

This journey to the Cross that we're taking together could use an occasional detour through more dangerous territory. I'm not suggesting that anyone put themselves in physical danger, but I am recommending some alternative activities and ways of thinking that bypass our comfort zones, that put us at dis-ease and that challenge our tendency to avoid anything costly. How else will anyone whom we come in contact with truly know what it means to follow Jesus? Ask God to challenge you today.

Prayer: Use us, God of the oppressed and repressed, to communicate your radical message of redemption and your costly message of sacrifice. Amen.

DISCOVERING WHAT GOD WANTS FROM US

Read John 16:13-17.

"When the Spirit of truth comes, he will guide you into all the truth; for he will not speak on his own, but will speak whatever he hears, and he will declare to you the things that are to come" (v. 13).

I remember reading a book several years ago that was advertised as the definitive resource necessary for any Christian to discover God's will. By the time I had finished reading it, I was so confused that I could barely pick out a pair of pants without wondering if I had the right style or color according to God's plan for my life!

It doesn't have to be that hard. I often identify two potential approaches to the basic question of guidance. The first is that God has a perfect plan that takes into account every possible permutation, every eventuality, every accident, or every potential choice we could possibly make, extrapolating from the infinite range of variables that might potentially come into play. We, then, straining to review or preview all of these details, must choose whichever direction fits best with our understanding of God's perfect plan. We either get it right, or we get it wrong. That's not only a lot of pressure but also sounds exhausting!

The second approach would be to get to know God more deeply, more honestly, more completely, and to yield ourselves to the Way. Paul suggests that we "with unveiled faces, seeing the glory of the Lord as though reflected in a mirror [spend time in the presence of Jesus], are being transformed [in response to the time spent with Jesus] into the same image from one degree of glory to another" (2 Cor. 3:18). Additionally, as Paul reminded his readers, "where the Spirit of the Lord is, there is freedom" (verse 17).

Freedom! If we are guided by the Spirit of Truth, then we are no longer in bondage to the obsession of trying to figure out the correct response to every possible decision, whether big or small. Instead, as Christians being transformed into the likeness of Jesus, Paul instructs us to "let the same mind be in you that was in Christ Jesus" (Phil. 2:5). Now that really is freedom.

FOLLOWING THE JESUS WAY

"Jesus said to him, 'I am the way, and the truth, and the life. No one comes to the Father except through me" (John 14:6).

"I am the way; I am the truth." If we are guided into truth, then we are guided into Christ. If we're looking for an encounter with God, and in so doing become transformed, more and more like Jesus, then we really are walking in the truth, walking in the light, and walking in the will of God.

I'm not convinced that God worries about the details we tend to get so bent out of shape about. I'm not sure that God is interested in telling us what town we should live in, the career path we should chose, or even what particular person we should marry. I'm more inclined to believe that God is more interested in being with us—period. Regardless of whatever circumstance we get wrapped up in, God wants faithful disciples who will live according to the law of love. That's how we become more like Jesus, transformed into the likeness of the Son. That's how we're going to follow more nearly.

Prayer: "Day by day, dear Lord, of you three things I pray: to see you more clearly, love you more dearly, follow you more nearly, day by day." (Richard of Chichester)

Day Twenty-One: Monday

POP QUIZ

Read John 16:17-20.

Then some of his disciples said to one another, "What does he mean by say-ing to us, 'A little while, and you will no longer see me, and again a little while, and you will see me'; and 'Because I am going to the Father'?" They said, "What does he mean by this 'a little while'? We do not know what he is talking about" (vv. 17-18).

Okay; pop quiz time:

Question: What did the disciples say more than almost anything else (other than "Who remembered to bring lunch?") during their three years of ministry and travel with Jesus?

Answer: "Huh?" "Duh?" "Run that by us again," and "We don't under-stand what the Master is saying."

That said, we really do have to give the disciples some credit. This was two thousand years ago and their world was very flat—perhaps almost two-dimensional in every regard. Everything they understood was clearly defin-able in terms of "This is what we see," "This is what we feel," "This is what we have been taught is true," and "This is what we can know experientially."

DEVELOPMENTAL MILESTONE

Developmental psychologists identify an observable landmark in a child's learning known as "conservation." Put a rattle in front of a baby and the infant will reach for it. Move the rattle, but leave it within the field of vision, and the child will still reach for the toy. Place the rattle out of sight under a blanket, though, and the toy has essentially fallen away from the infant's experience; the child will not reach for the object because—to the child—the rattle simply does not exist anymore. At an early developmental stage, there is no "knowing" for a child without a direct connection via the five basic senses.

Conservation means to conserve the image or the possibility of the desired object even when it has been hidden. At some point in development the child will continue to feel around for the rattle even when it is hidden from sight—understanding that it is still there, even though it is beyond the parameters of his or her five senses.

Likewise, it was often a real struggle for the twelve disciples to grasp Jesus' teaching because he referred to a world that was beyond the scope of their language or their experience. Traditionally, God had performed mighty acts, discrete and measurable, in history, in real observable time and space. Jesus, however, was talking about the spiritual world, of going away and of coming back, of sending another Comforter.

I believe it was to the disciples' credit that they didn't just swallow every ounce of this stuff hook, line, and sinker. They were willing to ask questions.

WE TOO CAN ASK HARD QUESTIONS

Jesus is still willing for us to ask questions of all sorts, hard ones and more basic ones too. Our God is not so small that we cannot sit back and legitimately wonder sometimes. In fact, the more neatly wrapped and tidy my God becomes, the more I have diminished the idea of deity through my small imagination and my profound lack of faith.

I know this much in the realm of conservation. "I am not ashamed, for I know the one in whom I have put my trust, and I am sure that he is able to guard until that day what I have entrusted to him" (2 Tim. 1:12). What do you trust God for, that you mostly cannot see?

Prayer: You are huge and beyond pinning down, God. Sometimes your majesty and power and greatness seem beyond our ability to understand. Help us to keep our feet on the ground. Grounded, that is, in the experience of your generous grace. Amen.

NO ONE WILL TAKE AWAY YOUR JOY!

Read John 16:16-24.

"When a woman is in labor, she has pain, because her hour has come. But when her child is born, she no longer remembers the anguish because of the joy of having brought a human being into the world. So you have pain now; but I will see you again, and your hearts will rejoice, and no one will take your joy from you" (vv. 21-22).

I remember each detail so clearly. Father's Day, June 20, 1982, 2:45 in the afternoon. It had already been a long day, after what had been an endless night and an even longer morning.

What a roller coaster of feelings we both experienced. Rebekah and I were exhausted and spent, physically, spiritually, and emotionally. And, then, when we thought that we had nothing left, a baby was born, our first! Andrew Kemp Maul was as tired as we were and visibly upset at being disturbed so rudely. But he settled easily into his mother's arms and then mine, more than ready to get a little bit of rest.

INSTANT FAMILY

And there we all were, just a minute or two into this new life, a small family huddled together in the hospital room, united and bound in the fabric of joy. We knew that every minute of pain and anguish had been just a prologue to the unimagined gladness that was instantly ours.

Jesus uses this exact image, the picture of birth, to prepare his friends for what was about to come and what the Passion would mean for them and for the world.

"You are about to experience real pain," the Lord explains, "as well as genuine grief. You are going to weep and mourn while the world around you rejoices. But just imagine how difficult it is to give birth. Think about it; have you got that mental image clear? Now hold that picture in your minds: just like new parents throughout the ages of time, the anguish that you feel now is going to be nothing compared to the amazing joy of new life."

I can see Jesus pausing, waiting for the graphic image to sink in. "I am new life. I am the journey, the truth about life and existence itself. You are soon going to discover that the miracle of birth is not limited to the moment a child comes into this world. And it is going to be a joy that's all your very own! No one will be able to take it away."

Hold that moment, if you will. Recapture the instant you first held a newborn child in your arms—maybe your own; maybe a niece, a nephew, a neighbor, or the child of a friend. Consider your experience as a follower of the Way.

Now think back to when you first understood the message of Jesus as being uniquely for you. Do you have the picture? Jesus wants us to take hold of that wonder now; he wants us to hold his love and the promise of divine grace with such tenderness and such emotional clarity.

One of the wonders of children, newborn babies especially, is the magical ability they have to reconnect all of us with our own deep and vulnerable places. Are we willing to invite God into those places today?

Prayer: We know that in you our joy is made complete, God. Grant us the courage to become vulnerable in your presence so we can invite you into the deep places. Amen.

Day Twenty-Three: Wednesday

THE REDEMPTION OF PROMISE

Read John 16:21-27.

> "On that day you will ask nothing of me. Very truly, I tell you, if you ask anything of the Father in my name, he will give it to you. Until now you have not asked for anything in my name. Ask and you will receive, so that your joy may be complete. I have said these things to you in figures of speech. The hour is coming when I will no longer speak to you in figures, but will tell you plainly of the Father. On that day you will ask in my name. I do not say to you that I will ask the Father on your behalf; for the Father himself loves you, because you have loved me and have believed that I came from God" (vv. 23-27).

Think "priestly tradition." In Old Testament times, priests interpreted God's law on behalf of regular people; they were still doing this when Jesus came along. But even the priests were not equipped to handle the actual presence of God.

When Moses went up into the mountains to spend some time with God, he had to hide in a crevice in the rock face so that, when God walked by, he would not be struck dead by God's presence (Exod. 33:19-23). Then, when Moses returned to the children of Israel, the people couldn't bear to see the left-over evidence of God's glory shine from their leader's face (Exod. 34:29-35). So Moses had to put on a veil, in order that his people would be protected from the glory.

How complicated was that! It was like a reflection of the moon's borrowed light somehow remaining on another surface, well after the sun actually disappeared for the night. Still, it was too much for the children of Israel, and they had begged Moses to keep his face covered.

So along comes Jesus. "This is something you need to understand," he says. "I'm here today so that you don't need an intermediary any more if you want to access the Father. I'm not even saying that I will have to ask the Father on your behalf, to slip in a good word, so to speak. Not at all. I'm telling you to just go ahead and talk with God directly. Use my name as a good introduction—that much is very important—but go ahead and do your own asking."

That amounts to one amazingly remarkable truth! Prayer, without a priest, direct access to the living God. Why? Because Jesus provides the introductions; we have the status of his sisters and brothers.

Of course, that's exactly what God had intended all along. Back in the Garden, after Adam and Eve had sneaked some of the forbidden fruit, they're the ones who made the choice to hide themselves behind some bushes and away from God's presence. When God walked in the Garden, in the cool of the evening breeze, he expected to be able to have a conversation with his children. God wanted to experience a little tête-à-tête with the people he loved so deeply. We can imagine how disappointed and hurt God was when Adam and Eve drove a wedge between themselves and the relationship they were created to enjoy.

But the good news is this: because of Jesus, we can walk with God in the Garden once again. That, my friends, is a wonderful privilege.

Jesus went on to tell his friends that the time was coming when he'd tell them about everything in plain language; a message even they could not miss. That time was, I believe, his death on the cross, and that kind of plain language was coming within just a few hours. The most direct and unequivocal message Jesus offered was his most eloquent sacrifice.

And, grace upon grace, the result of such clear communication is the redemption of promise, a new relationship with God and the opportunity to make our way, one pilgrim step at a time, back to the Garden. Today, identify one such pilgrim step, then take it.

Prayer: No more veil. No more hiding behind the bushes. Lord, we are humbled by our admission into your presence, the redemption of promise. Sometimes we're tempted to wish that we would glimpse more of your glory than we can reasonably handle. Surprise us, Lord, but surprise us gently. Amen.

TEACHING AS PERFORMANCE ART

Read John 16:25-33.

> *"I came from the Father and have come into the world; again, I am leaving the world and am going to the Father."*
>
> *His disciples said, "Yes, now you are speaking plainly, not in any figure of speech! Now we know that you know all things, and do not need to have anyone question you; by this we believe that you came from God." Jesus answered them, "Do you now believe?" (vv. 28-31).*

Teaching, as most of us know, is not an exact science. Oh, we'd like to think that it is, as we're studying in the ivory towers at the teacher's college. Just do this, plus this, and then mix in a little of this, and voila, the little darlings will be eating out of your hands and they'll all become scholars.

Unfortunately, it never works out that way.

Those who have read the Michael Crichton novel *Jurassic Park* will understand the basic idea of chaos theory. In spite of all the safeguards put in place to contain the dinosaurs and to prevent them from reproducing, "nature finds a way." Simply put, chaos theory states that given the amazing number of possible variables (from small things, like the time of day or what I had for breakfast or if a fly happens to land on the end of your nose, to large-scale factors such as plane crashes, disease, or a natural disaster), there is no way to predict with 100 percent accuracy exactly what will happen if presented with a given set of circumstances (including even the measurable sciences of our physical world). This theory leads to statements such as, "Somebody sneezes in New York, and three days later there's a tornado in Kansas"! One measurable event affects the outcome of another measurable event—that much we understand. But, by the time just a few seconds have passed there is too much information and there are too many possible permutations and too many impossible-to-measure variables in play; and our ability to draw conclusions or make reasonable predictions is compromised to the point that chaos is always a possibility.

All this brings us back around to teaching, and why interaction with students in a classroom setting is always more of an art than a science. I used to tell student teachers that the classroom experience is 20 percent preparation and 80 percent theater. Although I would make that statement jokingly, given the unpredictable nature of the classroom—especially factoring in the humanness of the teacher, each student, the administration, and the families involved—the truth remains that teaching is, at best, a form of performance art.

Chaos theory is a purely statistical concept based on the behavior of physical objects that react according to the predictable laws of nature as best we understand them. Children, on the other hand, are people, and given the nature of free will, people rarely behave according to predictable "laws" and principles.

The disciples who followed Jesus—a dozen or so guys and the women who traveled with them—were Jesus' classroom. Training these folk had been a three-year process of mentoring, lecture, dialog, study, and practical experience. We have already discussed the tendency of Andrew, Peter, and company toward denseness, so I can imagine that Jesus experienced his share of "teacher exasperation." But I can also picture the expression on the Savior's face when his crew finally "got it," when they can say, "Now we know . . ." (John 16:30). This was important stuff, and it was (and is) imperative that disciples of Jesus understand not only the depths of Christ's love but also some of the theology and rationale behind it all.

It is also imperative that pilgrims today understand the deeper meanings of our faith. "Happy are those who do not follow the advice of the wicked, or take the path that sinners tread, or sit in the seat of scoffers; but their delight is in the law of the Lord, and on his law they meditate day and night" (Ps. 1:1-2). Think about how you are "getting" Christ's message today. How will you respond to the challenge?

Prayer: Guide our minds, Teacher Creator, and help us to understand the remarkable depths of your generous love for us. Amen.

TROUBLE IN THE WORLD

Read John 16:29-33.

> *"The hour is coming, indeed it has come, when you will be scattered, each one to his home, and you will leave me alone. Yet I am not alone because the Father is with me. I have said this to you, so that in me you may have peace. In the world you face persecution. But take courage; I have conquered the world!" (vv. 32-33).*

The cliché "It's a small world" has been used so often the idea is routinely accepted as fact. The truth, however, is that our world is vast and complex.

Even America by itself can be overwhelming. I remember my first trip on a Greyhound bus. I was nineteen and new to the USA. I traveled out from Philadelphia and up to Buffalo; across the Canadian border to London, Ontario and on to Toronto; then back to Detroit, Chicago, and shortly there-after lots of wide-open spaces, before coming to Minneapolis. Minnesota was followed by hundreds more miles of wide-open spaces, through North Dakota and eventually into Montana, first Billings and then Bozeman. I had the Simon and Garfunkel lyric, "gone to look for America," stuck in my head for weeks.

The actual road time on that trip added up to eighty-two hours. By the end I was, quite simply, blown away by the scope of the United States. There were stretches of North Dakota where the bus ran full tilt without deviating for several hours and with barely a change of scenery. America was so big that I could scarcely take it in.

Europe is quite the opposite but equally as impressive in its own way. As I write, our son, Andrew, is driving from Germany and through Switzerland on his way to Italy, a short trip in comparison to my Greyhound odyssey-on-wheels. A European trip covering the same number of miles as my drive would take someone throughout the entire European continent and deep into North Africa, or wind its way through the capitals of every major nation, experiencing condensed history, disparate cultures, and countless varieties of topography at a mind-boggling rate.

THE STRENGTH OF THIS WORLD

This world defines strength in terms of armies, resources, and authority: kings, dictators, heads of state, leaders of all variety; democracy, theocracy, republic, kingdom, federation; mighty armies, nuclear arsenals, aircraft carriers, fanatical fighters; incalculable treasure troves, powerful economies, offshore accounts, deep wells, deeper pockets; multibillionaire software executives; railroad barons; oil sheiks, financial empires; vast political systems, capitalism, communism, free markets.

This amazing world, with its collective resources and fragmented will, has evolved into an immense network of development, invention, poverty, abuse, learning, exploitation, opportunity, oppression, freedom, weakness, and strength. The application of technology has increased the scope of wealth and power, depleted resources, squandered fortunes, and created jobs, leaving economies strong—or reeling—at an impossible-to-quantify rate.

But take a look at the reach of Jesus: an upper room, a humble Savior, and one small band of followers. Jesus' followers, who were seated together around the dinner table, could see clearly the evidence of one of the most abusive and corrupt empires this planet had known to date. Caesar's empire had its iron fist clamped tightly around the tiny nation of Israel, with legions ready to implement the brutal *Pax Romana*. The power of global repression was firmly in place, but Jesus came to Jerusalem prepared to offer his followers a new and living way, a standard to carry that he would pay for with his blood, and the kind of peace that could neither be established nor removed by any authority of this world.

Today the world offers just as much danger and repression in its own amplified version of "In this world you will have trouble" (NIV).

Yet Jesus states, humbly, categorically, and with complete confidence, "But take heart! I have overcome the world" (John 16:33, NIV).

Prayer: "We shall overcome; we shall overcome; we shall overcome some day. Oh, deep in my heart, I do believe, we shall overcome some day." Thank you, God of our confidence, for the assurance of your Word. Amen.

WASHED IN THE WATER; TAKE HEART

Read John 16:29-33.

"In this world you will have trouble. But take heart! I have overcome the world" (v. 33, NIV).

My wife, Rebekah, tells the story of a woman who visited her office to talk about her anguish concerning her adult son. The man, who was past young adulthood and almost into middle age, would often disappear for days and even weeks on end. His precipitous slides into oblivion were frequent, but he would typically bounce back and return home for a while. There was substance abuse in the mix, in addition to the constant battle with his toxic antisocial behavior. For the mother, it always seemed there were more holes to dig out of, more heartache to endure, and ever-growing grief.

"I promise I will pray for your son," Rebekah told her. "And I'm praying for you too, because I know that you must be in real despair."

"Thank you," the woman replied graciously. "It's difficult, and we certainly do need the prayers. But I'm not in despair, you know. . . ." She lowered her voice, almost conspiratorially. "You see he's baptized, and I have faith that God's promises are vested deep inside him. Knowing that gives me so much hope."

I HAVE OVERCOME THE WORLD

Sometimes, I pray for the people who live inside the homes I walk past during my early morning, three-mile trek with Scout labradoodle. I cover the unknown occupants with prayer, giving the potential of their coming day to God's providence. It may be that a child had to step over the prone body of a drunken parent that morning on the way to the school bus; it's possible that there is going to be tension over a breakfast table or tears over a family member's struggle (much like the woman with the fractious son who confides in my wife). The residents may be facing unemployment, financial hardship, disease, or tragedy.

Despair, you see, takes its toll on all of us—not only the people we know but also those whom we may never meet. But on some level, I believe, there's a bona fide spiritual slugfest going on. Despair is not something we need to yield to without taking up the fight. Jesus' promise can serve as the weapon we use to tell hopelessness to take a hike, as we to turn our time and attention to the One who brings peace and victory and meaning. "Take heart!" he says. "I have overcome the world."

THIS IS A JOURNEY

Lent is a good time to take a close look at our personal spiritual journey and to consider what exactly was at stake (what exactly is at stake) when Jesus prayed for his disciples, got up from the table, made his way to the garden and—eventually—on to the cross.

"Take heart," I can hear Jesus saying, "because the victory has already been won!"

Each of our individual battles is being played against the same backdrop of the final curtain, with the same foregone conclusion. The victory has already been won. "Where, O death, is your victory? Where, O death, is your sting" (1 Cor. 15:55)?

"No, in all these things we are more than conquerors through him who loved us. For I am convinced that neither death, nor life, nor angels, nor rulers, nor things present, nor things to come, nor powers, nor height, nor depth, nor anything else in all creation, will be able to separate us from the love of God in Christ Jesus our Lord" (Rom. 8:37-39).

Walk through your neighborhood today. Pray for the people, house by house. Ask God's blessing in the name of Jesus.

Prayer: We have been washed in the water; we have been set free by the love of Jesus. Thank you, God, for this most welcome good news! Amen.

NOW THIS IS ETERNAL LIFE!

Read: John 17:1-5.

"This is eternal life, that they may know you, the only true God, and Jesus Christ whom you have sent. I glorified you on earth by finishing the work that you gave me to do" (vv. 3-4).

Wow! Talk about an incredible affirmation. Just in case there's any confusion as to what exactly is involved in the hereafter, Jesus clarifies things for his friends with this powerful promise and an explanation about what the idea of eternal life really means—both in substance and in spirit.

C. S. Lewis (one of my favorite authors) argues that hell is, quite simply, eternal life without the benefit of God (see *The Great Divorce*). Or, to put the idea another way, hell is exactly what people who have rejected God want to experience. The place achieves its unpleasant character, Lewis suggests, as people live out their personal desires and gratifications without the mitigating influences of love, of following Jesus, and of placing God at the center of their hopes and dreams.

Lewis's words ring true for me (as his writings always have). But now, rereading Jesus' definition of eternal life, I find myself even further convinced that the thoughtful Oxford don was right on the mark. Because, when Jesus talks of "knowing the Father," it conjures up a well-rounded image of heaven that far surpasses the shallow clichés we encounter that advertise easy, unchallenging, or problem-free living. You know, the kind of thing that promises day after day of sub-par golf or instant gratification or a trouble-free life or undisturbed tranquility—in other words, promises that look good only when viewed from the limited perspective of my self-oriented daydreams and self-focused, make-my-life-easy wishes.

But Christ's invitation is always a call to restoration, a call back into a life that's made abundant by what really matters, a call to return to the Garden. In essence, Christ offers an experience of "stepping back into kingdom life" so that we are continually granted the opportunity to renew our redemptive relationship with God. Christ offers us the opportunity to return to the state of being intended for us from the beginning of Creation.

HEAVEN IN MY IMAGINATION

I have this image in my head of an amazing heavenly library where thinkers like C. S. Lewis, Plato, the disciple John, and many others offer readings from their writings:

- a garden reading room where Saint Francis facilitates symposiums on simplicity;

- a lecture hall where the apostle Paul offers "Romans for Dummies," and John explains the nuances of his Gospel;

- a comfortable parlor where Graham Greene lectures on *The Power and the Glory,* and Abraham Lincoln shares some background from his Second Inaugural Address;

- an auditorium where George Frideric Handel sits at the organ, annotating a lively master-class with commentary on his *Messiah.*

But the key to life in heaven would be my unrestricted opportunity to know God! There would be unlimited time, deep understanding, and the means to engage in intimate conversation over long meals and good coffee.

The first step on this journey into eternity is to enter into the presence of the Eternal every day; to actualize the possibility of deeper knowledge by walking through the gate Jesus has already opened; and to accept, on an emotional as well as an intellectual level, this startling invitation to really live.

"I am the gate," Jesus said. "Whoever enters by me will be saved, and will come in and go out and find pasture" (John 10:9).

Prayer: We already knew about you, God of the deepest possibility, before we started to know you more personally. Please encourage us in the purposes that we live, and please teach us how to know you on a deeper level still. We would enter by the gate. Amen.

UNITY IN JESUS

Read John 17:6-11.

> *"All mine are yours, and yours are mine; and I have been glorified in them.*
> *And now I am no longer in the world, but they are in the world, and I am*
> *coming to you. Holy Father, protect them in your name that you have given*
> *me, so that they may be one, as we are one"* (vv. 10-11).

I've always enjoyed watching people. Sometimes I arrive at the airport early for a flight and have to wait; sometimes my daughter drags me to the mall and goes into one of those odoriferous stores that I can't stand, so I sit outside for a few minutes so I can breathe. Either way, the parade of people walking by makes the few minutes that I'm obliged to hang around worthwhile.

Sometimes (because it's fun!) I pass the time by categorizing the people I see milling about:

- "Not from around here."
- "Older than she dresses."
- "Retired schoolteacher."
- "Definitely a lawyer."
- "Beautician for sure."
- "Escaped from the children for the afternoon."
- "Not pleased to be shopping."

When things really get slow I've even been known to sort people by denomination:

- 🕊 "That one shops like an Episcopalian."
- 🕊 "Haven't seen a plaid shirt like that since last time I was in Wisconsin—must be a Lutheran."
- 🕊 "Would you look at the size of the cross around his neck? Assemblies of God for sure."
- 🕊 "Peace beads and a CROP Walk T-shirt? Gotta be Presbyterian."

But unlike me, Jesus was no casual observer. I am sure he looked around the room as he prayed, very deliberately, for each of his friends. None of this "all heads bowed and eyes closed" disassociation for Jesus. I'll bet he named them all, one by one.

Jesus was well aware of the characteristics that made each of his followers unique. He knew their personalities, and he understood that their individuality was what made them strong. And he was conscious too of the difficulties involved in blending such a collection of characters into an effective team.

And I am sure that Jesus knew exactly what he was doing and that he chose this group precisely because he knew them well. And they, in turn, followed the Lord because of the same thing. Remember how impressed Nathanael was that Jesus knew him? "Here is truly an Israelite in whom there is no deceit!" (John 1:47).

Jesus still knows exactly what he is doing—because he chooses us and because he knows us.

JESUS PRAYED FOR UNITY

Despite our obvious differences, we really are "one," as Jesus prayed—at least that's the idea. And this unity in the body of Christ provides the most compelling witness to the authenticity of the good news that we have at our disposal. I enjoy attending events where believers from all theological stripes celebrate the faith we have in common. Christianity is all about the saving grace of Jesus, the journey to the Cross (and beyond), and the imperative to share Christ's transforming love with this hurting world.

If there are any doubts, then listen again to the tone of Jesus' prayer. Jesus prays passionately for me, for you, for each one of us. "I am not praying for the world, but for those you have given me, for they are yours" (v. 9, NIV). Jesus focuses the startling authority of his personal prayer to the Father on our well-being—that's you and me. Jesus is praying for all believers throughout time, especially those today.

It's quite staggering to think about Jesus Christ himself, lifting each one of us before the Father. His prayer is earnest, ardent, and tender. When I read this passage I get the feeling that Jesus held the exact image of my family, and yours, in his mind, and that he thought about me as an individual, as well as about you, when he prayed.

Jesus really does love us. Pray, today, for unity in the body of Christ.

Prayer: I can only echo your sentiments, friend Jesus: Holy Father, unite us by the power of your name. Amen.

Day Twenty-Nine: Tuesday

THE FULL MEASURE OF JOY

Read John 17:12-19.

> *"But now I am coming to you, and I speak these things in the world so that they may have my joy made complete in themselves. . . . Sanctify them in the truth; your word is truth. As you have sent me into the world, so I have sent them into the world. And for their sakes I sanctify myself, so that they also may be sanctified in truth" (vv. 13, 17-19).*

One of my friends has a well-used caution he likes to repeat and does pretty much every other week or so in my Sunday morning, "Everyday Christianity" adult Christian education class.

"But we weren't there, were we?" he'll remind us. "We have no way of knowing exactly what Jesus [or Paul, or Mark, or John] meant when he said those words—other than the words themselves. We must try our best to respond to the text without inserting our own thoughts or motivations and ascribing them to people who are not our contemporaries."

I'm paraphrasing, but that is essentially the gist of his position. And he makes a good point: we must be careful not to make the Bible say what we want it to say, without regard to context or historicity or what we actually know from careful scholarship.

LIFE-BREATHED BY THE SPIRIT

And so we find ourselves confronted by another remarkable saying of Jesus, a passage rich and instructive on many levels. But let's read the passage with my friend's caution in mind and in light of this companion truth: The Word is a living document, inspired and breathed on by a living God; this living document is often quickened in our minds and hearts by the insistent urgings of the living Holy Spirit.

"But now I am coming to you," Jesus prayed, "and I speak these things in the world so that they may have my joy made complete in themselves. . . . They do not belong to the world, just as I do not belong to the world. . . . Sanctify them in the truth; your word is truth" (vv. 13, 14, 17).

Joy is one of those words that is thrown around easily and often in the weeks leading up to Christmas (see my book, *In My Heart I Carry A Star: Stories for Advent*). Yet joy in the context of faith doesn't seem to command all that much attention the rest of the year—and most especially during Lent, the season of self-examination. "Joy!" is far too exuberant a concept for many of us. It's more robust and intrusive than the terms we're comfortable using to describe the (ordinarily subdued) lives of faith we tend to lead.

When we consider the way our twenty-first-century society uses the word, I'm convinced that we misunderstand what Jesus meant when he spoke of "joy made complete," this "full measure" of joy (NIV). Based on contemporary usage we're likely to limit ourselves to images of uproarious laughter, back-slapping, playtime, and the extravagances of affluent American life.

Jesus talked often and genuinely about joy. But Jesus' take on "joy" was nowhere near our narrow definition. Although I'm convinced that Jesus was right at home when it came to parties and laughter and fun, that was not the context from which he spoke about joy. Instead he spoke from the context of his final, tense hours before facing a horrible death, which he knew was coming, about this "joy made complete." What in the world was he talking about?

YOU CAN'T HANDLE THE TRUTH

The kind of joy Jesus talked about had little to do with the inconsequential elements that we normally associate with joy, things like corny jokes, fancy possessions, power, frivolity, or amusing diversions. Instead, the joy that Jesus talked about did have—and does have to this day—everything to do with understanding and experiencing the possibility of an authentic relationship with the living God.

"I have given them your word," Jesus says, "and the world has hated them" (v. 14).

I detect here in Jesus' prayer a hint of inevitability, as if Jesus was not at all surprised that the world hates his disciples because of the truth found in God's Word.

"Sanctify them by the truth," Jesus continues; "your word is truth" (v. 17, NIV).

And there we find the crux of the problem: the truth is often too much for people. The devil, Satan, can be defined as much by the word "lie" as anything else (see Rev. 12:9); but God's word is truth. Evil's most insidious work is to confuse people by the misrepresentation of the truth, so that God's word is rejected even as they believe that they are being honest. And we are all complicit.

True joy, then, can be found only in the truth. That truth is God's Word. Only sorrow and futility are to be found outside of that truth. It follows that the full measure of our joy comes in knowing the truth more completely, in knowing God, and in allowing ourselves to be known and publicly identified by the truth.

Prayer: Teach us your way, dear Lord, so that we will be able to walk in the joy of your truth. Amen.

WHERE ETERNITY WASHES UP AGAINST TIME

Read John 17:20-24.

> *"I ask not only on behalf of these, but also on behalf of those who will believe in me through their word, that they may all be one. As you, Father, are in me and I am in you, may they also be in us, so that the world may believe that you have sent me. The glory that you have given me I have given them, so that they may be one, as we are one, I in them and you in me, that they may become completely one, so that the world may know that you have sent me and have loved them even as you have loved me"* (vv. 20-23).

Sometimes when life and work and people get a little overwhelming, I'll drive Rebekah out to the beach so we can enjoy one of those "seafood and sunset" experiences Florida is famous for. After a recent dinner on the beach, as we walked where the ocean laps against the land, I couldn't help but think about how—in Jesus—eternity washes into the edges of time. Christ is the interface of the infinite and the sublime.

Nowhere else in scripture is this phenomenon illustrated so clearly as when Jesus, limited by the confines of human flesh, prays to the eternal God on behalf of his very finite friends. "My prayer is not for [my disciples] alone," he prays, "I pray also for those who will believe in me through their message" (v. 20, NIV).

Slosh, splash, lap, lap—the tide recedes as the water throws itself against the beach.

I imagine that there had to have been tears in Jesus' eyes. There had to have been a catch or two in his breath. There had to have been a break in his voice. Jesus' prayer is poetically tender, compassionate, and completely empathetic.

The Lord loved this small group of people. I'm sure that he must have forged deep and personal friendships, because he is the author of relationship. God created us for the experience of community, for relationship to one another and relationship to the divine. Jesus, fully human and fully God, understood and desired both ends of the equation. For him, relationships must have defined both his complete humanity and his eternal intentions—as God—toward humankind.

Jesus, who declared "before Abraham was, I am" (John 8:58), also meets us concretely in the here and now. Our struggle to respond to eternity is revealed in the way we respond to Jesus in real time. Jesus, in turn, was (is) reaching out to us, individually, in this prayer, walking with us, as the Creator originally intended in the garden of Eden.

I love the way Jesus refers to those of us who are yet to come and the way he appeals to God for the opportunity to share his glory with us, the same way he trusts us with his Father's message of insistent love. I am grateful that Jesus expressed his intention to continue to teach us the truth about God, and that he understood the comfort and the promise involved in that more complete realization of grace: "That I myself may be in them" (v. 26, NIV).

It is more than fitting that Jesus' final words at that last meal with his friends were a prayer and that his benediction was a commitment to continue his task of making God's perfect love evident in this world. And Jesus promised that he would accomplish all of this through his ongoing investment in each one of us, in our friends, in and through each soul reading today. "That the love you have for me may be in them" (v. 26, NIV).

"See what love the Father has given us, that we should be called children of God; and that is what we are. The reason the world does not know us is that it did not know him" (1 John 3:1). Think abut the intimacy of Jesus' prayer. Now respond in kind, as you take a moment to talk with God.

Prayer: Your love is so great that we simply cannot contain it, God. We are overwhelmed and humbled by your grace. Amen.

Day Thirty-One: Thursday

LOVING OUT LOUD FOR GOD

Read John 17:1-26.

> *"Righteous Father, the world does not know you, but I know you; and these know that you have sent me. I made your name known to them, and I will make it known, so that the love with which you have loved me may be in them, and I in them" (vv. 25-26).*

Here's a useful question: Why does the church exist? What makes a Christian church different from any other organization that provides community and seeks to do good in the world? Jesus answered this question in his prayer found in John 17, when he suggested that the reason faith communities exist is to "continue to make [the Father] known" (v. 26, NIV). Jesus goes on to explain, "So that the love [of the Father] with which you have loved me may be in them" (v. 26). I wish I could paste a photo of my church home here in the text, along with our pastors and maybe some of the folk in my small group, because God intends to love out loud through us.

Jesus hits this theme fairly hard, quite often, and from a number of angles. It's one reason this entire passage (chapter 17) is so crucial. Jesus is talking about love, love in the context of knowing, and he suggests in a number of ways that authentic love is best experienced through interpersonal knowledge—that loving and knowing cannot be separated.

Perhaps one of the most effective ways of making God known is through self-giving relationships. Unfortunately, many "religious" people apply tremendous energy to "witnessing" via condemnation (not our job), conviction (the Holy Spirit's job), guilt, judgment ("God did not send the Son into the world to condemn the world," John 3:17), and general "holier-than-thou"-ness.

But Jesus talks about God's kind of love taking up residence in people, and he talks about it so much that it's impossible to miss the message that people are going to know we're Jesus followers by the love that we live out loud. Jesus wants to live in us, and he prays with real conviction that the love the Father has for the Son will also take residence in our very being. That kind of love is transformational.

A FILTER WE POUR OUR LIVES THROUGH

There's often a sense in which the church affiliation of a Christian (the Christian being me or you) is no different from any other social connection— no different than being a member of a golf club, or the gym, or some kind of service organization, or fraternal order. For example, in my community a number of people demonstrate their allegiance to a certain university via the particular colors they wear. They tend to get very excited on game days, peppering their conversation with references to their school, or wearing their colors or even their sweatshirts to church. They're not the least bit shy about letting the world know how faithful and committed they are to their schools. Their allegiance is, in many ways, a defining association. And to be honest, it's a lot easier to tell that some folk around town are "Gators" than to know if they follow Christ.

Transformational faith is not just one more affiliation. Transformational faith changes us completely, to the extent that God becomes a kind of filter that our lives are poured through. Transformational faith tells the truth about Jesus, and the truth is a defining love that lives in us so fully that it becomes an extension of the kind of love that equipped him to give everything.

That's the story Jesus told in the way that he lived love out loud. And the volume at which he lived it was deafening. Ask yourself this question: What allegiance will I advertise today?

Prayer: Please help me to live my faith with more transformational conviction, Lord. I want people to see you when they interact with me. I believe this is your plan for my life in your kingdom. Amen.

WHAT DOES IT TAKE TO SET A HEART FREE?

Read John 18:1-3.

> *So Judas brought a detachment of soldiers together with police from the chief priests and the Pharisees, and they came with lanterns and torches and weapons (v. 3).*
>
> *For freedom Christ has set us free. Stand firm, therefore, and do not submit again to a yoke of slavery (Galatians 5:1).*

The message, the Last Supper, the garden, the betrayal, the Crucifixion, and the Resurrection—there is so much packed into these three days with Jesus. And it's all part of the radical plan Jesus set in motion for our healing.

Sometimes healing requires a drastic intervention, something that turns everything upside down, In the garden of Gethsemane it looked as if the malignancy of oppression had gained the upper hand. But Jesus understood that once the powers of darkness made their ultimate move, the light of love would have the final word.

THE TRAIL OF THE BROKEN HEART

Recently, a routine, "let's take a look" examination of my dad's arteries unexpectedly turned into a major ordeal that illustrates just how wonderful and how difficult healing can be. The experience helped me to realize what needs to happen if we're ever going to manage the repair work necessary to move forward through Lent and on into lives of more focused faith.

I've seen pictures of blocked arteries before, but when the cardiologist showed us the images from my dad's heart catheterization that day, we were all amazed he hadn't already had a massive cardiac arrest. The doctor was surprised as well. There was 90-95 percent blockage in six significant arteries, and the arteries bulged like sausages where the blood couldn't make its way through.

Consequently, the doctor recommended immediate surgery. And, in case we harbored any doubts about how serious the situation was, the doctor told him, "If you don't have the surgery now, you will have a heart attack—maybe today, maybe later this week, or maybe next month. But to let you leave this hospital without surgery would amount to medical malpractice."

My dad still wanted time to think things over, until it dawned on him that he could have a heart attack while he was making up his mind. So my mum signed some papers, the surgeon scrubbed, and before we knew it we were holding dad's hand and praying with him before he was wheeled off for what turned out to be a long afternoon.

The surgery, normally estimated to take three to three-and-a-half hours, continued through the afternoon for well over five hours. When the surgeon came into the waiting area to talk with the family, he explained exactly why. My dad, it turns out, had a layer of extensive calcification and cumulative scar tissue completely surrounding his heart, the result of some previously undocumented infection or series of infections.

My dad's heart was, quite literally, encased in a shell. The surgical team had to work hard to make their way through the casing before they could repair the damage inside. It was as if they had to break open a walnut, and it took a long time.

"So," my wife, Rebekah, said to the doctor, with a faint smile, "you set David's heart free."

The repair work was extensive; the blockages were huge, and the risk of abrupt cardiac arrest imminent. But—and this is a critical observation—my dad's heart could not be repaired until it had first been "set free."

The message from my dad's open-heart surgery is at once overwhelming, challenging, liberating, fearsome, and wonderful—it's a lot like the gospel.

This time of the year, these days leading up to Holy Week and the celebration of Jesus' passion, provide the perfect opportunity for the calcified among us to do what it takes to invite Jesus to set our hearts free and to provide spiritual healing . It's the only way we'll ever make it all the way through Easter Sunday without losing our way.

Prayer: Today I'm willing for you to break open my heart, God. Remove the tough skin I have cultivated, the hard shell I use to protect my need from your healing touch. I know that my spiritual life depends upon it. Amen.

THE RIGHT IDEA—
THE WRONG MOTIVATION

Read John 18:1-14.

> *First they took [Jesus] to Annas, who was the father-in-law of Caiaphas, the high priest that year. Caiaphas was the one who had advised the Jews that it was better to have one person die for the people (vv. 13-14).*

Caiaphas, as high priest in Jerusalem, thought he was able to see "the big picture." In light of Jesus' growing popularity after raising Lazarus from the dead, Caiaphas had stated that it would be better "to have one man die for the people than to have the whole nation destroyed" (John 11:50). Unfortunately, this priest's idea of "the big picture" was skewed by politics. Ironically, Caiaphas was correct with his general assessment—it was better to have one person (Jesus) die for the many. But Caiaphas's vision was restricted by his worldview, and his judgment was constricted by his preoccupation with political expediency. He was right—kind of—but for all the wrong reasons.

Jesus spent the last week of his life in Jerusalem. Over the past few weeks we have been following along with much of what he shared with his friends on that last Thursday evening. But the pandemonium of the unfolding events had started the moment he set foot in the city the previous Sunday, a headlong rush that would culminate in the darkness of Good Friday and the startling light of Easter morning.

ENTHUSIASM AND FEAR

It turns out that Caiaphas was not the first person that week who spoke the correct words yet missed their true meaning. Many people in those teeming, cheering crowds of people who greeted Jesus during his Triumphal Entry had missed the true meaning of his coming, and they missed it in the "couldn't hit the broad side of a barn" category of misses. The Triumphal Entry showed all too clearly the potential of Jesus to attract and excite throngs of people who saw in him a political savior. The civic and religious leaders responded in fear to this political potential and the possible repercussions by the Romans.

Jesus shared their concern but for different reasons. He feared that a groundswell of emotional response—without the benefit of discipleship—would misinterpret his vision of God's coming kingdom. Good grief, even his closest friends had had a hard enough time grasping his teachings clearly! But, as for the high priest, Caiaphas feared the opposite; he feared that the crowds really would understand this teacher. He feared a shift in focus from the requirements of the law to the requirements of love, and that simply would not do.

Of course, Caiaphas seemingly never grasped the true, spiritual implications of the teachings of Jesus; consequently, the idea of thousands of impassioned followers scared the living daylights out of him. Such a danger simply had to be stopped; such unrest might bring down the ire of Rome and cost the Jewish leaders what little autonomy remained in the midst of a harsh Roman regime. In short, the message Jesus was teaching might cost Caiaphas his comfortable livelihood.

Obviously, this view wasn't really based on Jesus' teachings and actions. But didn't they all notice that this "potent threat" rode into town on a donkey, a symbol of peace? Didn't they understand the Lord's utter indifference to the power structures and influence games that always seem to define our misguided planet? Hadn't they heard about the pain Jesus felt when he looked over Jerusalem, considered Israel's separation from God, and wept?

Instead, to the Caiaphas way of thinking, the death of Jesus was a bone to throw the Romans, a demonstration that the Jewish religious leaders were committed to peaceful coexistence. It was a way not only to save lives but also to consolidate the tentative hold the ruling class had on power. Therefore, Jesus was led to his death as a lamb to the slaughter; pure Passover blood was splashed across the doorways of believers; and a new world of possibility opened up, that promised freedom and liberty to every inhabitant on the face of the Earth. In effect, the result was the revolution that the leaders had hoped to avoid, but on a scale not even Rome could hope to oppose. It was danger unimaginable. . . .

In what ways do you feel liberated by Jesus? Make a list and share it with a friend.

Prayer: If I can ever understand the extent of your love, Lord, I will find the words to thank you. If I can ever bring myself to follow you with courage, Teacher, I will embrace the danger of discipleship. If I can ever pick up my cross, Jesus. . . . Amen.

ARE YOU ONE OF THIS MAN'S DISCIPLES?

Read John 18:15-18.

> *Peter was standing outside at the gate. So the other disciple, who was known to the high priest, went out, spoke to the woman who guarded the gate, and brought Peter in. The woman said to Peter, "You are not also one of this man's disciples, are you?" He said, "I am not" (vv. 16-17).*

We live in a day and age when there's a lot of confusion about what it means to be a Christian. The fact is that many people believe they have good reason to steer clear of religion. The term *Christian* has been associated with so much hypocrisy and so many carnival acts and so much public indecency that on one level I'm inclined to sympathize with those who turn away without so much as a second thought. Our job—our great opportunity as twenty-first-century disciples—is to do such an outstanding job of representing the authentic Christ that the cynicism of those who reject Christianity loses its potency.

Once in a while, when I'm traveling or at a party, I'll introduce myself to someone as a "Jesus-follower," a moniker intended to allay the "knee-jerk" closing of minds and hearts that describing oneself as a Christian sometimes causes. Then (usually in response to "a Jesus what?" or, "What do you mean by that?"), explaining what I mean by such a statement becomes less intimidating or sanctimonious or obnoxious.

PETER—"NOT ME, NO HOW, NO WAY. . . ."

The disciple Peter made a big show of saying he was not a disciple of Jesus; it's right there in today's scripture. But I believe Mr. Rock (see Matt. 16:18) often gets a bum rap for this statement, especially in light of the remarkable insight and enthusiasm that characterizes his witness the rest of the time. For all his bull-in-a-china-shop passion, his inconsistency, his impulsiveness, and his tendency to blurt things out, in the long run Peter turned out to be a sensitive, thoughtful, and courageous leader in the early church.

Yet this is the incident he's probably most famous for!

WATCHING IT ALL UNRAVEL

The evening Jesus was arrested—right after enjoying supper together in the upper room—it must have seemed as if events were descending in a downward spiral for the close-knit group of friends. Just a few days earlier they had felt so "up," so popular, so on top of the world. The Triumphal Entry into Jerusalem must have seemed like the crest of a new wave. But that wave quickly dashed against the rocks of disappointment, and now the disciples' lives were spinning out of control.

Peter—especially—had always been so sure and so confident. He wore his heart on his sleeve. And for good reason. Up to this moment, Jesus had been immune to the maneuverings of his opposition. He had outsmarted his detractors, healed the sick, challenged conventional wisdom, and taught so convincingly that anything and everything had seemed possible to his excited followers. Anything, that is, but betrayal and arrest.

Of course, Jesus had spoken clearly about the possibility of betrayal and death. More than once Jesus had spoken about the future, and he'd even told his friends flat out that he would eventually be arrested, condemned, and killed. But Jesus' warnings were a truth they really did not want to deal with—and so they managed not to hear him. This man was going to redeem Israel! This man was their Messiah! Those expectations didn't add up to anything near what Peter was experiencing the night Jesus was arrested, the night things started to unravel, that terrible night in the high priest's courtyard.

But the fact has to be faced: Peter and the other disciples still had not managed to grasp the essential idea of Jesus' teaching. Jesus was not concerned with creating a "successful" movement according to the world's definition of the word *winner*. Instead, he was intent on redefining a whole bunch of words, like *revolution, kingdom, peace, freedom, abundant life,* and *victory*.

Maybe, at some level, Peter was telling the truth there in the courtyard. Maybe at that moment he really wasn't one of Jesus' disciples. Maybe, when the girl asked him the question, he wasn't following Jesus at all. Maybe Peter was thinking something else, something like, *What can I possibly do for a dead leader?* or *How can I follow someone who is not going exactly where I want to go?*

It's quite possible that Peter's denial wasn't made from fear. Instead, it's possible that he was disillusioned and confused. I've been there myself. I think we all have. And we already know the rest of the Easter story.

Confused or not, take some time to contemplate and to talk with a friend about what it means to be a modern-day disciple.

Prayer: Purposeful God, please visit us with your spirit of assurance and encouragement. It is still all too easy for us to tragically misunderstand your message. Amen.

YOU CAN'T HANDLE THE TRUTH

Read John 18:19-24.

Then the high priest questioned Jesus about his disciples and about his teaching. Jesus answered, "I have spoken openly to the world; I have always taught in synagogues and in the temple, where all the Jews come together. I have said nothing in secret. Why do you ask me? Ask those who heard what I said to them; they know what I said" (vv. 19-21).

As Peter and the Beloved Disciple were waiting in the courtyard, Jesus was being dragged into a "kangaroo court" where his accusers could yell at him with impunity and try to justify their actions. But Jesus, when asked about his teaching, challenged the high priest's motives for asking and suggested that they question the crowds. Jesus pointed out that he had done nothing in secret. John picks up the story:

"When he had said this, one of the police standing nearby struck Jesus on the face, saying, 'Is that how you answer the high priest?' Jesus answered, 'If I have spoken wrongly, testify to the wrong. But if I have spoken rightly, why do you strike me'?" (John 18:22-23).

Jesus spoke the truth, which is what he always did and which is exactly why he was hit in the face. The official did nothing more than act out what many frustrated people desire to do when they are confronted with the truth of their actions—he lashed out. No one present could come up with anything in Jesus' actions that was actually illegal, and when Jesus pointed that out emotions ruled and there seemed nothing else to do but to hit him. I can imagine the high priest's police stamping their feet, raising their voices, and lashing out because they couldn't bully Jesus without him turning it into some kind of lesson.

When I taught in the public schools, I encountered a lot of children who responded just like that official. Unfortunately, I know a bunch of adults who react like that too. Because—and we all know this deep down—there is no antidote to the truth, just as there is no darkness that can possibly eradicate light. Jesus stood in what had become a dark place, and the light of his incisive truth was simply too much for them to deal with.

WITH JESUS THERE ARE NO SECRETS

When questioned, Jesus immediately reminded his accusers about the openness in his ministry, and openness is inherent to light and truth. Everything about his ministry was open and available to inspection, a fact evidenced by the number of people who were always welcomed and encouraged to ask questions. Even when Jesus was teaching directly to his close-knit group of disciples, there was often a fair crowd gathered, looking on, just to listen and to learn.

There was a fair crowd of people at my church yesterday morning. There always is, and I am sure that some who showed up were a little like the high priest's officers—not only curious but also looking for a reason not to believe. You know what I mean because we've all been there. Too much truth makes us nervous, so we find fault with the truth-teller, change the subject, or lash out in frustration, trying hard to be mad about something so that we can avoid dealing with God's kind of truth.

But Jesus understands. "Please," he invites us, "tell me what it is that is wrong." But at the same time he is not willing to let us off the hook. No, facing the truth is too important for that, and things have gone too far for that kind of a graceful exit! Because his truth is designed to expose our lie, his presence reminds us the extent of God's commitment to our healing, and his light illuminates our need for the kind of grace God always has in mind.

Caiaphas, the high priest, passed up another golden opportunity to learn from the Savior and instead sent him on his way to the Cross. There is always the danger that we will do the same. What truth is Jesus confronting you with today? Will you be transformed? Or will you simply strike out and turn away?

Prayer: Please don't let us off the hook either, Lord. Don't leave, just because we are so nervous. Expose our need with the light of your truth and then heal us with your grace. Amen.

UNTIL RECENTLY, DEAD!

Read John 12:1-11.

Six days before the Passover, Jesus arrived at Bethany, where Lazarus lived, whom Jesus had raised from the dead. Here a dinner was given in Jesus' honor. Martha served, while Lazarus was among those reclining at the table with him (vv. 1-2, NIV).

Today we're going to step out of the time-line sequence of the Gospel story. But it's a deliberate move—because The Greatest Story Ever Told is being told for a reason. I want to reexamine the setting for Holy Week.

For me, the reason for the story of Holy Week always comes into clearer focus when I think of my family. I know I write about my children a lot, but my experiences with them tell the story of redemption and reconciliation so clearly that I can't help but listen.

Recently, my daughter, Naomi, and her husband, Craig, came home for a week to celebrate my birthday. It would have been great to have our son, Andrew, in the mix too, but traveling from Tuscany is more of a challenge than from Connecticut, and Rebekah and I were going to be heading his way before long.

My birthday celebration was a long affair, during which we ate a large dinner together. But the repast—as in bread, wine, lasagna, chicken Parmesan, cannelloni, spaghetti, coffee, chocolate cake, and so forth—only constituted a small part of the occasion. Love and presence, not food, held sway over the evening.

AT TABLE WITH JESUS, LIVING AS IF WE MEAN IT

And so today we're jumping back to John 12, the story of Jesus attending a dinner party in Bethany. It's the day before his Triumphal Entry into Jerusalem. This time the meal is more like a deep breath, a last moment of tranquility before Jesus purposefully walks into Jerusalem to experience betrayal and a violent death. There is peace around the table—good friends hanging out, enjoying one another's presence. And look who's there! Lazarus, who until recently, lay dead in his tomb!

The Easter story is all about living completely, radically, and consummately; about living out loud, living as if we mean it. That is, after all, why Jesus was willing to go to Jerusalem and to give up absolutely everything for the people who were reclining with him around the table. He is still most welcome—not as a guest but as family.

Celebration is incomplete any other way.

DON'T JUST DO SOMETHING; SIT THERE!

Sometimes we find ourselves in such a hurry to extract all the meaning possible from this time of the year that we forget to sit at the table with Jesus and to just be. Jesus and his friends simply enjoyed the meal in Bethany. For Lazarus the joy was in being alive.

So I'm interested in a Lenten experience that for today at least puts "being" ahead of "doing." Many of us frantically "do" faith, showing up for every event at church, throwing ourselves into service and mission, tuning in to Christian radio in our cars. We try hard to live the practical expression of a holy life.

That's fine. But what are we doing about *being* holy? I believe that we should sometimes ground our experience in a spiritual practice that invites an attitude of "don't just do something—sit there"! Or, to use a phrase that my wife, Rebekah, often employs, "Everything we do at this church comes out of worship." And our worship would certainly benefit from a little more "Be still and understand the presence of God" as the impetus for the "doing" part of our faith journey.

BEING MOVES US INTO DOING

Such a vital experience of being propels us into action, action grounded in a more vital connection to "the source of all being." God, in my experience, is interested in occupying every element of our experience. The Creator doesn't just give us marching orders at church and check off what we're up to—God wants to inhabit our being and transform the experience.

In Mark's account of the "parable of the sower," Jesus pointed out that life can—and will—get in the way of the message when we forget to be still.

"Some folk are exposed to God's words; but then other—more pressing—priorities crowd their lives and get in the way. Eventually the message is pretty much lost to them. God's voice is choked out, and people receive no benefit from the transformational life it offers" (Mark 4:18-19, author's paraphrase).

Prayer: We know how important it is to be still and tune in to your voice, God. Help us to reprioritize and schedule more time at the table with Jesus. Amen.

> *There is a river whose streams make glad the city of God,*
> > *the holy habitation of the Most High.*
> *God is in the midst of the city; it shall not be moved;*
> > *God will help it when the morning dawns.*
> *The nations are in an uproar, the kingdoms totter;*
> > *he utters his voice, the earth melts.*
> *The Lord of hosts is with us;*
> > *the God of Jacob is our refuge.*
>
> *Come, behold the works of the Lord;*
> > *see what desolations he has brought on the earth.*
> *He makes wars cease to the end of the earth;*
> > *he breaks the bow, and shatters the spear;*
> > *he burns the shields with fire.*
> *"Be still, and know that I am God!*
> > *I am exalted among the nations,*
> > *I am exalted in the earth."*
> *Psalm 46:4-10*

SCRIPTURE = TRUTH = STRENGTH

Read John 18:25-38.

> *Jesus answered, "My kingdom is not from this world. If my kingdom were from this world, my followers would be fighting to keep me from being handed over to the Jews. But as it is, my kingdom is not from here" (v. 36).*

> *"I am not asking you to take them out of the world, but I ask you to protect them from the evil one. They do not belong to the world, just as I do not belong to the world.*
> *"Sanctify them in the truth; your word is truth" (John 17:15-17).*

These two scriptures worked their way into my brain this morning as I drove away from the airport. I got up extra early today to take our daughter and her husband over to Tampa International so they could board their flight back to Connecticut and home.

Sometimes, when Naomi and her brother, Andrew, were growing up, I really did pray that God would insulate my children from the world. Like Jesus, I wasn't asking God to whisk them away from the world as much as I was asking God to "protect them from the evil one."

To be honest, their civil liberties and freedom of choice were not exactly number 1 on my list of concerns as a parent. I would have been more than willing for God to bend the rules and intervene to keep them safe—with or without their consent. "Just get them grown, Lord," was my wife's and my constant refrain.

But God respects our freedom of choice—not only during those turbulent formational years but also throughout our lives. Intellectually, I understood that being "sanctified in the truth" was not something that could be imposed by outside forces. "Here, let me sanctify you in the truth—hold still, it's not going to hurt. . . ." It simply doesn't work that way. But, emotionally, I wanted God to skip the free-will part and simply ride herd over my children's lives.

Instead, and with faith, Rebekah and I had to watch and pray—in much the same way that God watches over God's children—and we all have to do our best to make sure that the truth is evident and authentic and accessible. Freedom is just one of the necessary building blocks to wholeness. Providing guidance, setting a good example, and (most importantly) teaching all play their part. But the moment we take away freedom, we also take away the possibility of legitimate growth.

Years of pain and struggle and heartbreak have yielded to joy. Andrew and Naomi are both young adults, and they are freely choosing the kind of positive courses of action we would have imposed on them as teens had we disregarded their free will (and, believe me, I would have done so if I had the power of God). Instead, by respecting their freedom, we allowed them to emerge from their growing understanding of truth and develop the strength of character that defines them today.

Jesus pointed to God's Word as truth. The power of evil is resourceful; but God's Word is a sword more than equal to the task. It is imperative that we immerse ourselves in truth so we are more than ready to take our stand when the time comes. How might you use scripture as the sword of truth today?

Prayer: Jesus walked this earth well armed with truth. Challenge all of us, great God who always teaches, to likewise prepare ourselves for anything that may come our way. Amen.

Day Thirty-Eight: Thursday

IMAGINATION

Read John 18:28-40.

> *"For this I was born, and for this I came into the world, to testify to the truth. Everyone who belongs to the truth listens to my voice." Pilate asked him, "What is truth?"* (vv. 37-38).

Jesus was in the business of challenging and changing people. At the heart of his message was this foundational idea that crops up time and again: "I was born . . . to testify to the truth."

It's a tantalizing refrain. But the way Jesus proclaimed his relationship to truth made people uneasy, especially those people in power. Sometimes it makes me uneasy as well. Because by offering truth, Jesus isn't offering anything according to the standards or the expectations of this world. In offering truth, Jesus expects us to change. "As it is, my kingdom is not from here" (see v. 36).

How might we have responded if we had been there to hear Jesus' proclamation of truth?

I've often imagined myself in Israel, on a dusty hillside in Galilee, just outside Capernaum, maybe just before Jesus made his way to Jerusalem. I am part of the multitude but on the edge of the crowd, just watching, happy simply to see the Savior (if only from a distance). I envision a rocky vista, some sparse vegetation, a smattering of grass—alive but pretty much blown brown by the dry wind. [I've been to Galilee, so I know what the topography looks like and I know the way it feels to be in that place.] The very boulders I leaned against may be resonating still with the distant echo of the great Teacher's words.

It's a large crowd—maybe five thousand people or more—stretching across the natural amphitheater created in the hollow of the hills, there above the brilliant blue sea. In the distance, around what can almost be described as a grassy place, near where a spring emerges from the rocks, the crowd is more concentrated.

I wander through the crowd a little, improving my position so I can see where hundreds of people are pressed together around the place where Jesus is sitting. Jesus is laughing softy, dangling his legs from an outcropping, and speaking quietly yet with the kind of authoritative tone that carries beyond mere volume.

Closer in I can make out the group of those who travel in the Lord's entourage. Then, closer still, his disciples—a dozen or so men and a handful of women—leaning in, deeply attentive, literally touching his garment . . . his arm . . . the bottom of a foot.

Out at the rim of the congregation, poised on the margins, half in, half out of earshot, scores of hesitant people are milling around. Some of them edge in and take a few tentative steps toward the man who is the distillation of their hopes and dreams (if only they would dare to trust him). But they waver, maybe turn around; maybe listen, maybe not.

I find myself wondering where I would fall among such a multitude. I wonder and then—if I wonder long enough—this is what I see.

IT GETS PERSONAL

I see a figure approaching—he's about six feet tall and of average build—long strides hurrying up the hillside as if anxious not to be too late. I see the cloak pushed back to reveal wavy, blond hair (I was blond once, and I still could be—at least in the summer) and brown eyes, piqued with curiosity, peering intently as the long legs stalk around the borders of the crowd.

And I watch this man stay, right there on the periphery, as if he—as if I—know exactly what will be required if he dares move any closer to Jesus. And I hesitate; I turn back; I stumble. Yet, still I do not leave; I cannot. What should I do?

The danger and the challenge of change hold me back, as they have always done. It's so comfortable here on the margins, looking in and listening to such fine stories, witnessing miracles, cheering Jesus along as he challenges the status quo.

But not my status quo.

And so I hold back, even though I know that the peace Jesus offers is nothing like the peace the world gives. But you see, the thing is, I'm used to this kind of peace, this level of predictability, this quality of challenge. So I wait, and I watch.

Prayer: God of imagination, of history, and of this particular day, accompany us on our pilgrimage to the Cross. Amen.

WERE YOU THERE?

Read John 19:1-18.

Now it was the day of Preparation for the Passover; and it was about noon. [Pilate] said to the Jews, "Here is your King!" They cried out, "Away with him! Away with him! Crucify him!" (vv. 14-15).

My wife, Rebekah, tells of a story she first read when it won a competition in the 1970s. She didn't have the original, but the essential theme concerned a period in the future when people could travel through time and were able to experience living history for educational vacations. What follows is based on that original concept.

The family in question had narrowed their choices to several key events. One child wanted to attend the Battle of Hastings in 1066; another was interested in the Mayflower landing in the New World. Finally the family settled on "Jerusalem and the Crucifixion of Jesus" in the year 33 CE as their "Destination Vacation."

So the family entered a chamber with around 100 other travelers and a guide. In preparation they were given special pills that somehow changed their physical appearance and language to that of the indigenous population (in this case, natives of the ancient Middle East). They were also provided with appropriate clothing and therefore were dressed accordingly.

"It is critically important," the tour guide explained, "that we all fit in. Under no circumstance should your behavior deviate from that expected during this period of history. It could be dangerous to stand out in the crowd."

The tour guide went on to detail several specific examples, including the crowd response and the call for the release of Barabbas. "No matter what your personal feelings dictate," he said, "you must shout out, 'Crucify Jesus!' along with everyone else."

Once in Jerusalem, the travelers found themselves carried along into the marketplace with a huge throng. They noticed that many people were also congregated in doorways, shops, and alleys, looking at the growing crowd with suspicion and something resembling fear. The visitors observed the way these people were acting with the feeling that something didn't feel right. But they all knew how important it was to fit in with the crowd, so they went along with the instructions. Still, something about all those people cowering in the shadows nagged at their minds.

Before long, some soldiers arrived, dragging a man who the visitors guessed was Jesus. He was shoved out in front of a pale, pudgy character, who looked significantly unnerved. The man—evidently governor Pontius Pilate—waved his hand dismissively and there was a hushed silence. All was quiet across the square; you could have heard a shekel drop. The time travelers glanced at one another nervously, waiting for something to happen. Then, suddenly, fearful that they may be exposed and mindful of their instructions, one of their group yelled out, hesitant but clear, "Crucify him!"

The cry actually sounded out of place; it was too soon. So, quickly, the rest of the group joined in, and before more than a second or two had passed, the entire crowd picked up the cry.

"CRUCIFY HIM! CRUCIFY HIM! CRUCIFY. . . ."

It almost sounded as if the cry was rehearsed.

With an awful shock, the vacationing family realized exactly what was happening. The marketplace was packed, yes, but not with locals circa 33 CE. Most of the indigenous population—residents of Jerusalem and those visiting for the Passover—were hiding in the shops, crowded into alleyways, or watching from the doorways. The square was actually crowded with thousands of time-travel tourists from the future. Each traveling group had been instructed, carefully, to respond in the same way. Their group was just one of many, from many times and places of origin.

"It's us!" one of the party whispered hoarsely; "We're the ones who are crucifying Jesus!"

What a stunning indictment! Yes, it was us. Yes, it is us. In a sense, we really were there. Jesus went to his execution with our shortcomings in mind—yours and mine, our broken relationship to eternity. Jesus suffered because of our separation from God. He died with our names on his final breath. What connection do you feel to the cross?

Prayer: We're just so grateful, Lord, that you are more grace filled than we are worthy. Amen.

CAUGHT IN THE SHADOWS, DRAWN TO THE LIGHT

Read John 18:1-10.

> *Then Jesus, knowing all that was to happen to him, came forward and asked them, "Whom are you looking for?" They answered, "Jesus of Nazareth." Jesus replied, "I am he." Judas, who betrayed him, was standing with them. When Jesus said to them, "I am he," they stepped back and fell to the ground. Again he asked them, "Whom are you looking for?" And they said, "Jesus of Nazareth." Jesus answered, "I told you that I am he. So if you are looking for me, let these men go" (vv. 4-8).*

Late yesterday afternoon, my wife went out into the garden for a stroll while I got busy in the kitchen with some fresh vegetables and another recipe from my newest cookbook. It was a beautiful afternoon, sunny and clear. Our garden is a serious mess right now and needs some work, but here in Florida that's not stopping the early roses from blooming. They push their way out regardless, full with the promise of summer and bursting with hope.

So Rebekah snipped a delicate bud and brought it inside to sit in a vase on the counter top. This morning, as I ground the coffee, I saw that the rose, caught in the first rays of sunlight, had opened all the way.

WILDERNESS AND REDEMPTION

One dominant theme of the observance of Lent for the church has always been the idea of wilderness. The forty days of Lent are a period of spiritual renewal related to the forty days (a long time) that Jesus spent in the desert, wrestling with his purpose and preparing for public ministry. Sometimes there's a run at self-denial as we try to enhance our personal spirituality by moving away from pleasure or distraction. I understand what's behind this way of thinking, but I believe it's uncreative to mistake routinely grey tones and solemnity for truth about God.

Tomorrow—Palm Sunday—marks the beginning of Holy Week, but today's scripture comes from the Gospel of John's account of the night Jesus was betrayed and arrested. The Temple guards came bursting in through the dark night in a move designed to intimidate Jesus and the disciples. They expected to find fear, panic, and running away. Instead they came across Jesus, calm as you like, not going anywhere. When Jesus asked these rude intruders who they were looking for, they answered, "Jesus of Nazareth."

Jesus stood in that dark place (like the rose Rebekah discovered in our garden), blooming his heart out, catching and distilling the light, calling people to shift their focus toward the morning. It's a provocative thought to consider, most especially given the fact that the gang who came to arrest him were, like millions of others throughout history, also "looking for Jesus." Caught in the shadows; drawn to the light.

THE SEARCHING HEART

I've never really thought about it before, but the tragically confused, the angry, the criminal, the hateful, the misfits, the lost, and the resentful among us are looking for Jesus. Jesus recognized this in those who came to arrest him, and he was willing to meet them exactly where they were. Jesus always is.

Christ blooms with beauty and clarity wherever we may need him: in a run-down garden, an oppressive workplace, a broken relationship, a lost life, an abandoned faith, or whatever form our Gethsemane takes. Jesus blooms there because he understands the searching heart. Even when we're at odds with everything—maybe especially then—Christ does not leave us, because God is always ready to be found when there's a search on.

I love the way Jeremiah expressed this principle: "I will let you find me, says the LORD, and I will restore your fortunes and gather you from all the nations and all the places where I have driven you, says the LORD, and I will bring you back to the place from which I sent you into exile" (Jer. 29:14).

"I will let you find me, and I will restore your fortunes." That's what Jesus' point is. That's the message of the rose. It's the message of Gethsemane. It's the message of Holy Week for each one of us, every time and in every season.

Back from exile. When you walk into church tomorrow, imagine that you are coming home.

Prayer: Today we'll listen to God: "For surely I know the plans I have for you, says the LORD, plans for your welfare and not for harm, to give you a future with hope. Then when you call upon me and come and pray to me, I will hear you. When you search for me, you will find me; if you seek me with all your heart, I will let you find me, says the LORD, and I will restore your fortunes and gather you from all the nations and all the places where I have driven you, says the LORD, and I will bring you back to the place from which I sent you into exile" (Jer. 29:11-14).

Day Forty-One: Palm Sunday
RIDING HIGH ON A DREAM

During Holy Week, we're going to follow Jesus' last few days of ministry in Jerusalem. So today's reading jumps back to the beginning of that fateful week.

Read John 12:12-19.

> "So they took branches of palm trees and went out to meet him, shouting, "Hosanna! Blessed is the one who comes in the name of the Lord—the King of Israel!" . . . The Pharisees then said to one another, "You see, you can do nothing. Look, the world has gone after him!" (vv. 13, 19).

Palm Sunday is one of my favorite mornings to attend church. Every year without fail an unruly mass of children marches into the sanctuary, waving palm branches and singing as loud as they can. They tug at my heartstrings. Maybe it's the way they toss the huge palm fronds about in time to the music (older worshipers are always warned to sit a few seats in from the center aisle), or maybe it's the looks on their faces, the pure radiant light, as they sing enthusiastic praises.

Even the most reluctant children, who start out slinking their way in, dragging their branches ("I'm only doing this because I have to!"), can't help but fall into the spirit of the occasion once they make it halfway down the aisle.

Likewise, I can imagine how excited Jesus' followers must have been that first Palm Sunday.

"Whoo-hoo! We've finally made it to Jerusalem!"

"This is what we've been waiting for!"

"It's going to be nothing but smooth sailing from here on."

"Look at Jesus! That's *my* Savior and friend!"

Even the religious leaders, those who had been plotting to get rid of Jesus, were overwhelmed at the critical mass of popular support the upstart teacher mustered that day. "The Pharisees then said to one another, 'You see, you can do nothing. Look, the world has gone after him'!" (v. 19).

It doesn't surprise me that feelings were running so high. The disciples were coming to Jerusalem directly from the dinner party in Bethany, where they'd enjoyed the company of a group of friends and supporters that included Lazarus, the man Jesus had raised from death! (John 11).

But Jesus wasn't riding any wave of emotion, nor was he caught up in the ecstasy of the moment. No, the Lord did what he always did: he identified the powers and the priorities that define this world and he faced them head on. Jesus may not have been looking for a confrontation—but he did absolutely nothing to avoid one when it materialized. Jesus was riding a donkey, the symbol of humility, into the midst of the rising storm; I can imagine that he was calm, serene, confident, and unfazed by the danger.

Celebration is a simple statement of spiritual truth.

I don't believe any of the disciples had fully allowed the euphoria of that first Palm Sunday parade to blind them to the harsh reality that they faced on a daily basis. Life was still difficult; Israel was still an occupied country; and poverty and disease were still rife. But Jesus was reorienting their perspective and now, for the first time, they were beginning to grasp the fact that they had a future and that they most certainly had a hope.

Sometimes—especially right in the middle of struggle, uncertainty, tension, and stress—it's a good thing simply to celebrate, regardless of the circumstances. The wonderful truth is that we know Jesus; we know the rest of the story; we know how wonderful it is to live a life of exuberant faith; and we know how much God loves us.

There's no denying how difficult it is to maintain optimism and hope in the face of tough times. But Jesus is our anticipation and our expectation, and so we're not exhibiting a simplistic, pie-in-the sky hope for the future when we celebrate. The Christian celebration, as exemplified by our Palm Sunday worship services, expresses a statement of a spiritual truth.

So let's all go nuts today! Let's wave the branches and sing the songs! Let's not allow any petty things to come between our great need and the life-giving affirmation of Jesus. We celebrate a Savior who rides into town on a donkey, because the way of the Cross is always the way that is unexpected.

Prayer: Thank you, God of life-changing stories, for leading us through a time of reflection and into the powerful culmination of Lent. Accompany us on our journey through Holy Week, the passion of Jesus, and into the joy of Easter Sunday. Amen.

PUSHBACK

Read Luke 20:9-19.

When the scribes and chief priests realized that he had told this parable against them, they wanted to lay hands on him at that very hour, but they feared the people (v. 19).

Palm Sunday launches us into Holy Week with real momentum, drive, thrust, and energy. The definition of momentum—if I remember my high school physics correctly—is mass multiplied by velocity. And Luke's account of the events leading up to Good Friday comes hard and fast, offering both spiritual gravitas and a purposeful sense of high-speed action.

In yesterday's reading we witnessed this dynamic burst of energy and excitement as Jesus wowed his way into town. From the perspective of Matthew, Mark, Luke, and John, Jesus took Jerusalem by storm. But hopefully Christ will rock our home communities too as we live out the powerful effect the edgy teacher must always have on those with ears to hear.

Given the circumstances—enthusiastic crowds, energetic songs, bright clothes, springtime optimism, and the carrying of gospel truth into the heart of the city—and the setting—Jerusalem, where power brokers set up shop and made their dangerous alliances—it was only natural that the powers that be would eventually push back; and they sure did.

THE OPPOSITION TAKES IT UP A NOTCH

I wonder where the pushback is hitting us today—you and me? According to Luke's telling of the story, a cascading sequence of events takes place Monday through Thursday. Jesus tells the truth, and the pushback seems to build with each new day. In the following excerpt from Luke's narrative, Jesus tells a lightly cloaked parable of the present reality:

> Then the owner of the vineyard said, "What shall I do? I will send my beloved son; perhaps they will respect him." But when the tenants saw him, they discussed it among themselves and said, "This is the heir; let us kill him so that the inheritance may be ours." So they threw him out of the vineyard and killed him. (Luke 20:13-15)

It turns out that the momentum that has been building around Jesus' message and mission was not an irresistible surge toward peace and love or hugs and flowers in your hair. Instead, Jesus has set into motion a series of events challenging the status quo that will inevitably result in death. Pushback is most insistent when there is a threat to status quo, when the values that define a culture are so obviously upended, when the truth demands that the current crop of power-peddlers be replaced with new gods—in this case, the one true God.

So this week I have been asking people to think about the call to be revolutionary in our own culture. Not to be rude, not to be overbearing, not to be holier-than-thou, and certainly not to be disruptive for its own sake. But—alternatively and no less subversively—the call to be revolutionary is a call to be authentic and conscious witnesses to the truth in all that we do. By doing so, we will not only make obvious to others that our values are the values of Jesus but also (in our way of being) subvert the "gods" our culture has previously chosen.

OUT THE DOOR

The parade of children that bounced its way into my church the morning of Palm Sunday has turned into a parade of people going back out into the world just a short hour and a quarter later. We sang; we celebrated; we prayed; we read God's word; and we listened to the good and challenging news of the gospel. But then we were called to leave the church and to be followers of the Way in this world.

We're carrying the same message that Jesus offered, the message that led to the cross. Aren't we? How will the Jesus story be told in our lives today?

Prayer: I cannot carry more, my God, than fractured splinters from your cross. Give me the courage here, I pray, to honor you, embrace the cost. Amen.

WHAT YOU SEE
IS WHAT YOU GET

Read Luke 20:20-26.

So they watched him and sent spies who pretended to be honest, in order to trap him by what he said, so as to hand him over to the jurisdiction and authority of the governor. . . . But he perceived their craftiness. . . . He said to them, "Then give to the emperor the things that are the emperor's, and to God the things that are God's" (vv. 20, 23, 25).

"I give you a new commandment, that you love one another. Just as I have loved you, you also should love one another" (John 13:34).

I have penned a paraphrase that I like to use for verse 23: "Jesus saw through their duplicity."

I have a question. Ready? Okay, here goes: what do Rebekah (my wife), Naomi (my daughter), and Scout (Rebekah's fuzzy, galumphing, seventy-five pound labradoodle) have in common? (Warning, this is a hard one.)

First off, they're all girls! Right. But that was the easy answer.

The characteristic I'm getting at would be fairly obvious if you knew them. Each has a pure, "what you see is what you get" approach to life. Put another way, there's not an ounce of pretense among them.

This means they don't "play games." Yes, Scout likes to play "tug the rope" and "chase the dog if you ever want to see your wallet alive again"; and Naomi's pretty good at pool, but those are not the kind of games I'm talking about. What I'm talking about is their lack of duplicity, their "let's not waste time with airs and political correctness" approach to life, their "cut to the chase, why don't we?" response to almost everything. (Okay, Scout likes to play chase but that's something else too.)

It's an approach to life with not only a kind of purity but also more, like the gift of living without half measures or enjoying relationships without the cloudiness of compromise, or resisting the urge to allow cynicism any room at all.

It's about authenticity. It's about being real.

THE JESUS WAY TRUMPS FRAUD

Jesus knew that role well; he did not have one iota of interest in playing games. Consequently, he was always able to see right through the kind of people who would posture, feign, practice treachery, or outright lie. Because these kinds of people expect others to be just like them—mistrust breeds mistrust—Jesus' straightforward approach and refusal to play games always threw them. The Jesus Way always does.

Liars have a hard time dealing with people who hold to the truth. Truth exposes liars and makes them nervous, so they don't like it one bit. The sad thing about their mistrust is that the truth also has the capacity to heal, to love, and to set people free. But—and we'll go back close to the beginning of John's version of the Jesus narrative for this one—people who choose to deal falsely (to operate in the dark, as the Gospel of John puts it) are in fact pretty much scared of the light of truth.

"This is the verdict," John writes. "Light has come into the world, but [people] loved darkness instead of light because their deeds were evil. Everyone who does evil hates the light, and will not come into the light for fear that his deeds will be exposed" (John 3:19-20, NIV).

Those who were trying to trick Jesus could not begin to understand the Savior. They had a value system with firmly set filters, and the truth simply could not and would not resonate in them. But understanding Jesus isn't really possible outside of surrender.

THIS IS THE WORLD WE LIVE IN

We all encounter agitators like those we read about in today's reading, people who are not content to quietly disbelieve but who advance an aggressive, anti-Jesus agenda. But the proper response isn't to condemn them or to learn how to argue them into submission with logic or to fall into the trap of cynicism or to respond in kind to their toxic way of understanding the world.

The proper response is to love people the way that Jesus loved them—the way that Jesus loves us. Love is our mandate. Loving others as Jesus loves us won't necessarily make things any easier, but it will say something critically important to this world about the kind of God we profess to follow.

Prayer: We're so grateful, God, that love was the mandate of Holy Week. You gave everything to offer us the chance to experience the kind of wholeness we were created for. It is an opportunity we embrace with humble thanks. Amen.

THE GREATEST STORY EVER TOLD

Read John 19:13-19.

> *So they took Jesus, and carrying the cross by himself, he went out to what is called The Place of the Skull, which in Hebrew is called Golgotha. There they crucified him, and with him two others, one on either side, with Jesus between them (vv. 16-18).*

> *"For God so loved the world that he gave his only Son, so that everyone who believes in him may not perish but may have eternal life. Indeed, God did not send the Son into the world to condemn the world, but in order that the world might be saved through him" (John 3:16-17).*

I always have a difficult time thinking of what to say or to write about the crucifixion. I've heard preachers elaborate on the pain Jesus experienced, preach volumes on how the soldiers cast lots for Jesus' seamless garment, and wax eloquent regarding the way the great Teacher was concerned about his mother in spite of his own suffering.

When the movie *The Passion of the Christ* was released several years ago, someone gave my wife and me tickets to an advanced screening. We talked about it and initially decided to go, although we remained apprehensive.

I have always had a problem with graphic violence. I understood the educational rationale for the opening scenes of *Saving Private Ryan*, which portray the first wave of the Allied invasion at D-day; and I grasped the purpose behind the director's documentation of the horrors of the Holocaust in the movie *Schindler's List*. Even so, I waited a long time before viewing either movie, preferring to screen them at home.

I'm not suggesting the producers exploited the explicit violence of the Crucifixion merely for entertainment value and to sell tickets (which is often the reason for including violence and which is inappropriate on many levels). Certainly history has documented the story of the brutal *Pax Romana* in excruciating detail. "Where they make a desert," Tacitus wrote, "they call it peace." Cruelty was without a doubt common enough during Jesus' day and thus a dimension of the Easter story.

One evening, as we were eating dinner before the screening, Rebekah put our apprehension into words. "Why would I want to spend two hours," she said, "watching someone I love so much being tortured and killed?"

The amazing reality for me, in considering the horrors of that day, is that Jesus not only knew exactly what was going to happen to him, but also could have ended it at any time. He could have stopped the Crucifixion at a moment's notice, before they jammed the thorns into his head, before he was forced to drag the heavy cross along the Via Dolorosa (the Way of Suffering), before the next nail was cruelly driven in. Yet he chose to see it through.

I'm still a little stunned by the implications of those violent acts of cruelty and hate. Because the horror of what Jesus experienced puts the ball squarely in my court.

Without that day, I can listen to Jesus teach, and I recognize his wisdom; I can even intellectualize his message. I can hear of his miracles and compassion and help with my money and time. I can witness his ministry to the downtrodden, the rejected, and the dispossessed; and I can be encouraged along my own pilgrim path. I can play my guitar in worship, and I can teach my heart out, and I can facilitate small groups and train leaders and so much more. And I can avoid most of the emotional baggage that getting too close to real life can rattle loose. Without that day, I can keep my spiritual life as neat and clean and controlled as I like.

But the Cross! The Cross forces me to confront the harsh realities of my own journey and my separation from God; it forces me to admit to the real cost of my self-centeredness and my closed heart. The Cross of Jesus demands an emotional response, and I'm not so sure of what to do with that kind of Savior.

ANTIDOTE TO EVIL!

To be honest, somewhere inside of me I would prefer that Jesus had not died; I would be more comfortable with the idea that he had negotiated our salvation and sponged up my shortcomings with his good deeds. Sometimes I cannot stomach the idea that anything about me might have been part of what placed someone like him on a bloody cross. It just isn't right, and I feel that I want him to take my guilt away.

However, what occurred on the cross two thousand years ago is the only effective antidote to evil that I know. That is the heart of the story. Not Roman brutality, not Jewish culpability, not my squeamishness—and not any other distraction that people who are nervous about the idea of God want to talk about instead of the difficult truth.

THE GREATEST STORY EVER TOLD

What Christ achieved by being born voluntarily into this world as a child, living his life with fullness and in joy, and willingly going to the Cross, has to be The Greatest Story Ever Told. It's a story that penetrates all my defenses and a story that resides in every crevice of my heart.

Truth like this threatens "the way things are" on so many levels that controversy, hostility, and disbelief in response to it come as no surprise. I simply pray that my life—and yours—"shine like stars in the universe as [we] hold out the word of life" (Phil. 2:15-16, NIV). And that, because of the way we engage this story, the message gets through.

Imagine how you might retell the story to a friend who has never understood it. It's your story now, and the world needs it still.

Prayer: Sometimes we are overwhelmed with sadness at the events of your passion, Jesus. Please speak the truth through our lives, this week, and help us to share the story via the manner in which we remember. Amen.

THE GIFT OF PRESENCE

Read John 13–17.

> *Now before the festival of the Passover, Jesus knew that his hour had come to depart from this world and go to the Father. Having loved his own who were in the world, he loved them to the end (v. 1).*

John 13–17 comprises five complete chapters; and, yes, we have already covered most of the text a passage at a time. But today, Holy Thursday, I'm recommending a rereading of the entire narrative of that last evening in one sitting to provide a feel for the collective weight of all that Jesus said and of all that transpired there.

Imagine the scene: a group of close friends, gathering together for dinner. Each of the official "Twelve" would have been there, and perhaps the women who formed a faithful part of the traveling party too.

First-class supper conversation is one of my favorite experiences. Good friends at table together, great food, and heartfelt dialogue that reflects both a shared history and the mutual love that we all feel are the ingredients for a meaningful experience. Rebekah and I have been privileged to share many such meals with our church family here at our local community of faith.

This particular evening with Jesus morphed into one of those experiences, during which the disciples learned more timeless truths from their Master. I imagine that Jesus was pensive, thoughtful, and more reflective even than usual. He was shouldering the load of the world's cumulative guilt on his heart, and it was beginning to show.

Jesus' mood certainly wasn't caused by fear, but Jesus must have felt a sharp uneasiness regarding what was about to transpire. If you read between the lines, you can almost feel Jesus reaching out to his friends and inviting them to help share this tremendous burden. But they simply weren't able to do so. They couldn't fully comprehend what was beginning to happen, and they could only follow Jesus when he went to the garden at Gethsemane later that evening. They remained pretty much clueless as always, pulling tentatively at the edges of his experience.

The result, of course, was that—for all intents and purposes—Jesus went to Gethsemane alone that evening. Physically, his friends were all there (even Judas, who arrived later), but Jesus bore the heaviness of the coming horror without the conscious support of his closest companions because they just couldn't bring themselves to believe.

I'd argue that we hurt Jesus much the same today, when we take the identical posture as his best and most faithful friends and skirt around the edges of what he is really up to. The events of Holy Week have serious consequences. Jesus knowingly walked into Good Friday, without hesitation, for each of us. Let us at the very least offer him the gift of our devotion and the clear evidence of our love.

GETHSEMANE

I have been to Gethsemane. To get there you cross the Kidron Valley to the base of the Mount of Olives and enter an ancient grove of olive trees. Scientists have dated some of the gnarled specimens at well over two thousand years of age. There, across from the old city of Jerusalem, I was able to sit on the stony ground and lean against an olive tree—a tree that Jesus himself may have leaned against on that awful, blessed night.

And today, sitting here at my computer, I like to imagine that—deep in the heart of that particular tree and resonating in the prehistoric stones—are the literal echoes of the Teacher's defiant, courageous words. Words addressed not just to the impulsive Peter but to all who listened then and who listen still, to every person willing to grasp the timelessness of God's intention and the integrity of Jesus' willing sacrifice.

"Am I not to drink the cup that the Father has given me?" (John 18:11). Jesus certainly did not want to experience the coming hours of pain, torture, and mortal anguish. But the deep power of his willing action is revealed in its incredible cost.

The young rabbi was not simply immortal God going on a symbolic jaunt to salve the legal sting of human rebellion. Not at all; Jesus was flesh and blood, human being—faced with the horror of torment, shame, and painful death. Jesus was and is God made flesh so that he could bear the burden of our shortcomings. And he did this voluntarily, with his eyes wide open, of his own free will.

What would you have prayed with Jesus if you had had the chance? Write down your prayer.

Prayer: Grieving God, grant us the courage to watch with you in the garden tonight. Amen.

COMPACT BENEDICTION

Read John 19:16-30.

> *After this, when Jesus knew that all was now finished, he said (in order to fulfill the scripture), "I am thirsty." A jar full of sour wine was standing there. So they put a sponge full of the wine on a branch of hyssop and held it to his mouth. When Jesus had received the wine, he said, "It is finished." Then he bowed his head and gave up his spirit (vv. 28-30).*

So far, this has been a week of amazing contrasts and eternal significance:

- Dinner in Bethany
- Triumphal Entry
- A week of growing controversy and tension
- A Last Supper
- Gethsemane
- Betrayal
- Arrest
- Questions
- Denial
- Trial
- Abuse
- Crucifixion
- Death
- Finality

"It is finished." This stage of the plan is now completed, achieved, accomplished, consummated, fulfilled. The iconic statement is Jesus' last deep breath, the kind you take after completing a long and arduous task. It is a successful conclusion, a shout, a punctuation mark in bold print. It is, in effect, a compact benediction.

COMPLICITY

Jesus' ministry here on earth had been remarkable to the extreme. His three years of public service were so crucial, so important, that he had spent thirty years in preparation. Thirty years! Thirty years of groundwork for the mission of Emmanuel, three decades of foundation for God Incarnate to get to work. Jesus did not rush into his ministry.

Therefore, as terrible as it sounds, Jesus' statement, "It is finished," serves more accurately as an exclamation point affirming that the Son had been completely successful in his mission, not as a concession to defeat. Because the moment Jesus died, the possibility of our redemption was born.

When Jesus uttered the statement "It is finished" on that Good Friday and it echoed across all of history, he opened the door of possibility so that we could be restored to God as if we actually were worthy. In fact, and because of Jesus, I really am worthy; we all are.

Regardless of how I understand it, that dark day on Golgotha saved me. The best I can do in response is to live in the truth of such generous love.

For me, and for each one of us, this life of redemptive grace made possible by the events on Good Friday has only just begun.

Prayer: Thank you, God, for giving us all a new beginning because of Jesus. Thank you for restoring us to the possibility of grace. Thank you for being willing. Amen.

WHAT GOOD IS A KINGDOM WITHOUT A KING?

Read John 19:31-42.

> *They took the body of Jesus and wrapped it with the spices in linen cloths, according to the burial custom of the Jews. Now there was a garden in the place where he was crucified, and in the garden there was a new tomb in which no one had ever been laid. And so, because it was the Jewish day of Preparation, and the tomb was nearby, they laid Jesus there (vv. 40-42).*
>
> *"But as it is, my kingdom is not from here" (John 18:36).*

Jesus was dead. There was no getting around it. Jesus' life was over. And yet there was no perceptible change in the state of things in Israel or in the world around him.

"But as it is, my kingdom is not from here."

Sometimes, I wake up to an uncommon stillness on Holy Saturday. The morning is heavy with a sense of finality, as if everything has come to a stop. The feeling is probably a cumulative Lenten response, exacerbated by the powerful effects of the Good Friday observance I attended at church the previous evening. I simply can't shake the gloom of the Crucifixion from my mind, and I'm not sure that I want to. I'm caught up in the stark reality of the Cross.

They freed Jesus' body from the heavy timbers of the cross. Some of his followers wrapped his body with spices and strips of linen, and then they sealed it in a nearby tomb.

"But as it is, my kingdom is not from here."

SOMETIMES, WE STRUGGLE

Recently, I had a day where I experienced something like the darkness that must have settled on the disciples that day after Calvary. In response, I tried praying, humming hymns, and talking to God about the emerging day. I went through the motions of morning devotions. I prayed again. But no matter what I tried, the sense of oppression pushed back.

Later, as I drove my car to a meeting, I abandoned my efforts to escape the feeling of darkness and instead embraced it. I thanked God for being so active in and through my life that "the enemy" felt threatened enough to attack me. Immediately, I felt a rush of peace replace my anxiety, and I thanked God for being with me in the middle of my struggle.

Then, as if on cue, when I turned on the radio the opening measures of a song came through and spoke to me: "Lord, make me an instrument of your love."

And suddenly I understood. God had allowed me to experience a period of darkness for a reason. Only by experiencing darkness do we realize how important this fight is; how far-reaching the repercussions are; what a tenacious enemy we have; and most importantly, what a gracious presence the Holy Spirit is willing to be, teaching us all we need to know in the Father's good time.

DEAD AND BURIED

Burials always have a stunning air of conclusiveness about them. So I can imagine the dark, empty emotions that Jesus' friends must have felt through that Friday night and on into Saturday. All around them, people were celebrating the Passover. But, for the followers of Jesus there was no festivity. Instead of passing over, the angel of death had visited them with devastation and finality.

"But as it is, my kingdom is not from here."

All of the hopes and the dreams for the future that had been kindled and nurtured through the past years had been wrenched from the cross and sealed in a cold tomb, a burial that signified the end of everything the band of followers cared for. Even more, Jesus was not only their hope for the future; he was also their best friend and their family. They had loved him, and now his life had been brutally snuffed out.

Their grieving carried with it fear and anxiety and doubts and soul searching. What should they do? Where could they go? Would their deaths come next? Or would they be such obvious failures without their Master that they would pose no threat and no one would even bother about them?

"But as it is, my kingdom is not from here."

What was the use of those three years of teaching? What about all Jesus' talk that "the kingdom of God is like" this or this? For that matter, what good is a kingdom without a king? And how could Jesus' friends possibly continue to do his work with their leader cold in the grave?

Such a day of desperation. Celebrate Passover? Not likely. If only this experience had simply passed them all by. It was left to Joseph of Arimathea and Nicodemus to take care of Jesus' body, because his disciples had crumpled, given in, and fled in their depression and fear.

That Saturday had to have been one of the darkest days in all of history. But only by fully experiencing that darkness can we fully experience what follows.

"But as it is, my kingdom is not from here."

Think about the kingdom that Jesus advanced. Where do you see it in evidence today?

Prayer: Even with our hindsight, Lord, we forget that your kingdom is not of this world. Show us your way and lead us into understanding. Amen.

EMISSARIES OF HOPE

Read John 20:1-29.

Jesus came and stood among them and said, "Peace be with you." After he said this, he showed them his hands and his side. Then the disciples rejoiced when they saw the Lord (vv. 19-20).

If Jesus' discouraged group of followers had been able to sleep at all that endless Saturday night after the long, stressful aftermath of crucifixion, they would have awakened to another new day facing the bitter pain of promise broken. Their defeat still loomed against the unremitting backdrop of disappointment, staleness, and death. Which is not surprising, given that they were still stuck fast in their "kingdom of this world" mind set. Only a stunning miracle could shake that limited ideology loose from its moorings.

And a miracle is exactly what happened! Jesus had demonstrated God's supremacy in the face of death, abandoned the tomb, and stood poised to move on to the next stage of his long-term mission here on Earth. Unfortunately, his friends were not yet ready to join him. John reports that they "rejoiced when they saw the Lord" (20:20), but you can be sure that they still didn't understand the truth of what was happening.

The bottom line is that the Resurrection was almost too much for the disciples. And who could blame the frightened group of men and women? So it took several encounters with the risen Jesus, over a number of days and in a variety of settings, before Peter and the rest finally understood Jesus' intentions and the next phase of the great plan.

UNSURE OF WHAT COMES NEXT

Once they grasped the overwhelming actuality of the Resurrection, the disciples were no doubt elated. The promise of life beyond the grave changed everything. But, as their actions and words indicate, they were still unsure of themselves, still doubting, and still fearful. Of course it was like a dream come true to see the Savior once again. But the followers of Jesus needed to understand that the kingdom Jesus was always talking about was not limited to the imagination, standards, and scope of the world they knew, understood, and were comfortable in. They needed to understand that Jesus the man would no longer be physically present to direct their activities, that Jesus' time with them had been only phase one of a greater, long-term, universal plan. In one sense, they had regained Jesus only to lose him again to a new role. "But as it is, my kingdom is not from here."

"Peace be with you," Jesus went on to say. And, "Receive the Holy Spirit" (John 20:21-22).

REDIRECT

So the stunning victory that amazing Easter morning did not verify the hope some followers held that Jesus would lead a popular campaign to free Israel from Roman oppression. There would be no hands-on, Jesus as point man, "see-touch-feel-taste-smell" movement. No army of excited followers; no triumphant "riding the coattails of God" in and through the physical presence of this risen Jesus. Not now, not ever. They simply had to realize that God's plan is far more involved and infinitely more far-reaching (the word *infinitely* here is used with care) than anything they had imagined.

"Have you believed because you have seen me?" Jesus asked. "Blessed are those who have not seen and yet have come to believe" (John 20:29).

In other words, the promises and the commission of Easter are placed firmly and squarely on us, you and me, God's twenty-first century Easter people.

"Peace be with you."

"Receive the Holy Spirit."

The joy and the excitement that we feel on Easter morning, as we dress up for church and sing the great hymns of praise, are real—there's no doubt about that! What we experience absolutely is the presence of the living Christ, right here with us in this day and this time. The truth of the thrilling miracle of Easter is that today, at this moment, we can know the grace and peace of a risen Savior!

God is not limited by time and space. We are called to be emissaries of hope and charged to carry this love and the living presence of life-changing, future-directing, world-saving redemption into this tragically broken world.

What a privilege! What a joy! What an awesome responsibility!

I wonder what might be next? What do you believe the Lord has in mind for you? Write a short list of ideas.

Prayer: We are most privileged and blessed, Lord, to know you in all of your resurrection power, and to enjoy that experience in a fresh way, today! Amen.

JESUS AS DESTINATION AND GUIDE

Read John 21:15-19.

Jesus said to [Martha], "I am the resurrection and the life. Those who believe on me, even though they die, will live, and everyone who lives and believes in me will never die. Do you believe this?" (John 11:25-26).

Welcome to the day after Easter.

If you attended church this past weekend, you were doubtless involved in a supercharged celebration. Such an experience always electrifies me, and come Monday morning I'm still filled with the life-saturated energy of the day. But I'm concerned that the charge I feel may be more a temporary, residual effect from the weekend than an active call to respond for today and on into the future.

My wife, Rebekah, used her Easter-morning message to discuss how quickly we tend to consign Jesus back to the tomb (where he can't bother us) and roll the stone securely back into place. Later, depending on how we're feeling at the time, we may open the sepulchre a crack and take a peek at the potential life that the risen Christ offers, but only once in a while. (I call this tendency the "Jesus as museum exhibit" syndrome.)

SPECTATOR OR PARTICIPANT?

The charge that we push Jesus back in the tomb (because he's a little too dangerous for our way of life) raises another question. Do we attend church each Easter merely to listen to the story of salvation, or do we attend to become active participants in that story?

134

The thrill we experience from the events of Easter morning may be growing harder to remember as the hours pass. But the initiative that Jesus launched through those events depends on our being open to God's Spirit as vital and real and relevant in everything we do in every moment of every new day.

Living our Easter faith out loud is all about getting the right start, and engaging each day as if Jesus really did defeat death and evil before leaving the empty tomb. It's about making sure not only that each day's trajectory is toward Jesus but also that it encompasses Jesus. Jesus serves as both destination and guide.

So I wonder, how will all of the details, concerns, deadlines, and conversations of my week be changed in light of the Easter truth I am called to proclaim? How will the story of my life be a witness to this truth today, next week, and during the coming year? Will I have the spiritual fortitude to keep the Prince of Peace not only on my mind but also in my heart, surrounding my actions? And I wonder, what will we do with this risen Lord?

TODAY IS THE DAY AFTER EASTER

Today is the day after Easter . . . or is it? *After* is such an unsatisfactory word when talking about everything that Jesus intended and accomplished through his heroic journey into the abyss. So I'm going to discard the word *after* and substitute an idea that I've been discussing a lot over the past few months: "Easter is the Eighth Day of Creation."

I've never been comfortable with the belief that God has stopped creating. Once, during a summer vacation, Rebekah and I were standing in front of Mount Saint Helens and looking into the remnants of the huge crater that had exploded in the spectacular eruption of 1980. As we watched, the mountain went "poof," a small cloud of ash launched into the sky, and we shuddered in deep respect. There's a new cone forming, and the mountain may eventually grow by another thousand feet or more. I realized then that God is constantly creating and renewing and imagining in this world. That's the kind of power that is released and can animate our lives of faith when we remember that we're Eighth-Day Believers!

And so the concept of God creating the world in only six days and then declaring, "I'm done," simply doesn't work for me. God's work in creation extends beyond the first week, and Rebekah's message that we're participants with God in that continual Eighth Day re-creation captures exactly what res-urrection is about. Participating in re-creation is essential to what being truly alive as followers of Jesus means. Rebekah's explanation dovetails perfectly in terms of where I understand this deliberate observance of Lent has been taking us.

TAKING THE NEXT STEP WITH JESUS

I never intended to wrap up this book and our observance of Lent on Easter Day, because I'm interested in where our Easter momentum is taking us. Eighth-Day believers live in the life-directing truth of resurrection. There's no tomb visitation any more. Now it's time for us to step forward and take part.

Easter Sunday was never our final destination during Lent. Easter Sunday is a triumph, yes, but it serves as an inspirational staging area for what comes next. If we leave the church as confirmed Eighth-Day believers, then what we're really doing is signing up to join Jesus in the re-creation business.

God is up to something significant, and we get to participate.

JESUS MOVED ON

Interestingly, the physically risen Jesus was only around for a few weeks. Before long the flesh-and-blood Jesus gave his final instructions, ascended, and was gone. Once Resurrection day initiated the new order Jesus moved on, because in part two of the plan the responsibility passed to, and remains with, his followers.

So today, the conclusion of our conversation together, is the perfect opportunity to begin seeing ourselves as Eighth-Day believers—followers of Jesus who are empowered by the living presence of the Holy Spirit. Otherwise we don't have a prayer of accomplishing any part of the amazing future that Easter Sunday makes possible.

We're no longer spectators. We're now participants in the new creation. If our journey through Lent together has prepared us for anything, then I pray it has prepared us for this.

Prayer: Easter is a huge idea, Creator God, when you recast the imperative of re-creation to bring the rest of us on board as partners with Jesus. We're both grateful and unnerved by the implications of resurrection. Help us to live fully in the truth of Easter triumph and by the power of the Holy Spirit. We ask in the name of the Christ, because all things are possible when we believe. Amen.

STUDY GUIDE

INTRODUCTION

Easter is a difficult concept for our secular society to grasp. Death and resurrection fail to fit our consumer mentality as easily as Christmas when it comes to commercial appeal. So, other than "giving something up for Lent," people tend to ignore the spiritual implications of observing the season altogether, or get sidetracked by the rites of spring and the gift-bearing Easter Bunny.

Christians struggle with how we observe Lent too, but for different reasons. We are often so preoccupied with day-to-day life that we don't make the time for daily practices that help us experience the deeper meaning of the season of Lent. So we gloss over the long hike between Ash Wednesday and Palm Sunday, and when Holy Week arrives we're not fully prepared and find ourselves out of synch with the sacred rhythms that make the church calendar such a great idea.

The following thought from day one, "Sacred Rhythm" (p. 12), speaks to the essential difficulty faced by twenty-first century believers, when it comes to fully engaging the potential spiritual journey that Lent offers.

> But Jesus' idea of freedom was problematic for more than just Rome; it disturbed many of his fellow Israelites too. Jesus failed to fulfill the "Conquering Warrior Hero" concept or to deliver the political freedom they sought. He spent three years explaining and clarifying what he meant by the phrase "kingdom of God," but the crowds kept looking for something more familiar.
>
> Today, like those early followers, we still tend to reinvent the character and the picture of the God we worship, so the image fits more tidily with the values and the priorities that define the culture in which we are comfortable.

It's not so much that we're afraid of the challenge as it is that we don't hear clearly enough. We're hobbled in terms of expectation. We have already decided (or it's been decided for us and we blithely go along) what it all means, and we only pay attention to whatever reinforces our preconclusions.

The Easter paraphernalia that the store displays "on Aisle 13" is only there because that's what people have come to think Easter signifies. The store displays eggs and chocolates and bunnies because merchants know we will buy them.

The unfortunate truth is that we, as a culture, are comfortable with secularization. And we believe that being "comfortable" is a worthy goal in life. Consequently, we like our religion comfortable too.

This study guide is offered as an aid for those who want to chip away at comfortable while moving steadily along the road less traveled. The goal is that, by the time Holy Week rolls around, we will be more intimate with Jesus, wrapped up in his challenging words, and more than ready to respond to the imperative of the Cross, the opportunity of resurrection, and the invitation to live as "Eighth Day Believers" who refuse to re-consign Jesus to the tomb.

There are essentially two ways to use the text as an ongoing Lenten study.

1. Take an individual journey

2. Meet with other people: believers and seekers alike

     ✺   in a traditional Sunday morning class

     ✺   in a Bible study class

     ✺   in a small group

     ✺   in a more casual gathering of friends

Reaching toward Easter works well as an eight-session study, or a meditative one-day-at-a-time resource, beginning the day before Ash Wednesday and running through the day after Easter Sunday. Each session references a set of readings, opens and closes with prayer, suggests questions for discussion and recommends an action plan.

READINGS

Fresh Eyes on Easter
Days 1–5

OPENING PRAYER

Bless this conversation with your presence, living God. Please take our intention to follow you seriously and encourage us each step along the way. We ask in the name of Jesus, who made today not only possible, but also full to the brim with possibility. Amen.

DISCUSSION QUESTIONS

- What is the point of Lent?

- If you plan to attend (or did attend) an Ash Wednesday service, how does the "imposition of ashes" affect you, spiritually?

- How is a sacred rhythm helpful to spiritual life?

- What are your expectations for this study between now and Easter?

- How have you experienced the commercialization of Easter?

- How will this study help you to keep your spiritual focus?

PLAN

- Read one reading from *Reaching toward Easter* each day through Easter Sunday

- Think about the idea of "an elegant, uncompromising invitation to live" (the reading for Day Three). Try to begin to implement abundant life as a spiritual discipline.

AFFIRMATION

Read the following, in unison: "I pledge to read at the very least the scripture selected for each day this week. I will ask God to shed the light of truth on every word and welcome God's presence in each detail of the unfolding day."

CLOSING PRAYER

Be our guide, Great Teacher, on this journey to Jerusalem. Teach us your way. Amen.

Session Two

READINGS

Days 6–12

OPENING PRAYER

Too often, God, we attempt to patch up the veneer of our spiritual lives without going beneath the surface where the real work must be done. Help us to clear away the debris of our distractions to the extent that the work of shoring up can get underway. We can only move forward from a solid foundation, and that foundation is Jesus. Amen.

DISCUSSION QUESTIONS

- Which event in the life of Jesus—birth through ascension—would you like to attend, given the opportunity? Why?

- What is one example of how God spoke to you through the scriptures this past week?

- If God does intend for us to live "as if we mean it," what might that signify for you?

- The reading "God-Saturated Behavior" (p. 40) finishes with a series of "what if" questions. Look these questions over, and discuss them with an open heart.

PLAN

- Continue to read, intentionally.

- Select someone in the study group to call during the week. Make the arrangements during this session, exchange phone numbers, and promise to follow up at least twice before the next meeting. On the phone (or over coffee), ask each other how the spiritual journey is going. Ask how you can pray for the other person. Follow through.

DOUBLE BACK

In the reading "If You Say That You Love Me" (p. 33), the author described someone who transcended the limitations of time and space in her spiritual life. Think about that for a moment, a quiet minute or two without conversation. Ask God to move you into a spiritual realm that is hard to quantify.

CLOSING PRAYER

Loving and challenging God, we all own a lot of "what if" questions. Grant us the courage and the will to move from the merely theoretical into the realm of practice. Be the God who restores. Be the God who moves. Be the God we dare to believe. Amen.

Session Three

READINGS

Days 13–19

OPENING PRAYER

We are conscious, God, of the freedom we enjoy to worship, to meet together, and to enjoy Christian community. So we pray for those who can expect an Easter celebration fraught with tension, threat, danger and persecution. This gospel is the only guarantee of liberty. Your truth is the only truth that sets people free. Your love is the only promise we can count on. Thank you for the unending gift. Amen.

DISCUSSION QUESTIONS

- Any road worth traveling comes at a price: conditioning, equipment, toll, commitment, tenacity, leaving things or people behind. To this point in your life, what have been some of the costs associated with your spiritual journey?

- How do you believe you would fare in a society intolerant of personal and corporate faith?

- To what extent is your Christian experience encouraged and supported by the faith community?

SCRIPTURE

"I have said these things to you to keep you from stumbling. They will put you out of the synagogues. Indeed, an hour is coming when those who kill you will think that by doing so they are offering worship to God. And they will do this because they have not known the Father or me. But I have said these things to you so that when their hour comes you may remember that I told you about them." John 16:1-4

- 🐚 What is there about Christ's message that could most disrupt the culture we live in?

- 🐚 What is Jesus saying to you "to keep you from stumbling"?

PLAN

- 🐚 Do some research. Find out some facts about religious persecution in today's world. Then pray for those brothers and sisters. Think about sending a letter of support and encouragement.

- 🐚 Consider living your faith out loud this week. What might that look like that's potentially different from "business as usual?"

- 🐚 Promise to pray for the person to your immediate left this week. Follow through.

CLOSING PRAYER

Gracious God, you are a "live-faith-out-loud" kind of God. We want to take this moment to declare our intention to be your "live-faith-out-loud" people. Make your presence an active reality in our lives as we take more deliberate steps to follow you. Amen.

Session Four

READINGS

Days 20–26

OPENING PRAYER

Your coming into this world as an infant opened up the promise of new possibilities, loving God. Your decision to take the journey all the way to the cross moved that promise into the realm of accomplishment. Be with us, we pray, as we wrestle with the idea of what it means to follow you with more purpose. Amen.

DISCUSSION QUESTIONS

- How has the birth of a child (possibly your own) helped you to understand more completely what it means when God describes us as "children"?

- Jesus was in the business (is in the business) of rebuilding relationships between people and God. How would you rate the quality of the relationship you have with God? What aspects about your relationship factor into your rating?

- The disciples were students in Jesus' "class." What is Jesus teaching you through this study?

- Think of a promise you learned from the Bible (look one up if you can't remember). How confident are you in God's promise? How is this journey to Jerusalem helping you interact with God's promises?

PLAN

- Read the scripture selections from this set of readings with extra care. Imagine taking what Jesus says seriously—believing the promises, acting on the words of Christ. God's Word becomes the living Word in and through our response to it.

🌿 Pray each day for those studying with you. Begin to translate what you are learning from Jesus into a kind of "prayer without ceasing."

TO THINK ABOUT

The reading "Washed in the Water: Take Heart" (p. 72) considers the promise inherent in baptism and its power over despair. How do you understand healing? When have you claimed a promise of healing?

CLOSING PRAYER

Taking you at your word is a big risk, Lord. Grant us the courage and the trust to live lives of more compelling faith and eloquent witness. Amen.

Session Five

READINGS

Days 27–33

OPENING PRAYER

Because of your great love, Jesus, we have been introduced to eternity. But we live in a here and now desperate for meaning and purpose. Be with us in our thinking and in our discussion, Lord. Teach us how to live in unity and to embrace your gift of abundant life. Amen.

DISCUSSION QUESTIONS

- Read the section "What Does It Take to Set a Heart Free?" carefully. Discuss the idea of a heart needing to be broken before it can be set free. What in this chapter resonates with you?

- Jesus referred to himself as "the gate." In what way has your relationship with Jesus served as an entry point for eternity?

- What makes "a Christian church different from any other organization that provides community and seeks to do good in the world"?

SCRIPTURE

"Righteous Father, the world does not know you, but I know you; and these know that you have sent me. I made your name known to them, and I will make it known, so that the love with which you have loved me may be in them, and I in them." John 17:25-26

- What would your faith community look like if "the love with which you have loved me [would] be in them, and I in them"?

- If you believe that Jesus intended "the world" to know "the Father" via the way believers demonstrate love, then what might that demonstration look like?

- Think of one thing that might be different in your life if you followed the wishes of Jesus.

PLAN

- Follow up on whatever came to mind in the discussion above.

- Expand your prayer commitment to include the life and work of your faith community.

CLOSING PRAYER

We have thought about some pretty big questions and challenges today, Lord. Be with us as we strive to follow through. Help us to understand what it is that you have in mind for us as we seek to follow Jesus. Amen.

Session Six

READINGS

Days 34–40

OPENING PRAYER

Sometimes we live too much in the shadows, God. But Jesus offers light and life. Animate our discussion with truth, we pray, and guide us into a deeper understanding of what it means to truly live. Amen.

DISCUSSION QUESTIONS

- Consider the following statement, "Jesus stands in the dark place, blooming his heart out, catching the light, calling people to shift their focus toward the morning."

- Does history judge Peter too harshly? How would you have reacted to such a challenge after Jesus had been arrested?

- In what ways does God add light to your dark places?

- In what ways is following Jesus like the morning?

- Think about how you are implicated in the death of Jesus; share one or two examples with the group.

SCRIPTURE

Jesus said to her, "I am the resurrection and the life. Those who believe in me, even though they die, will live, and everyone who lives and believes in me will never die. Do you believe this?" John 11:25-26

- 🕊 The Gospel of John highlighted a series of specific miracles. They come to a crescendo with the raising of Lazarus from death. What impresses you the most about the story of Lazarus being raised from the dead?

- 🕊 Talk about the difference between "spiritual resurrection" and "physical resurrection." Which do you believe Jesus is promising? Why?

- 🕊 Answer Jesus' question: "Do you believe [that those who believe in me, even though they die, will live, and everyone who lives and believes in me will never die]?" Explain your answer.

PLAN

- 🕊 Wake up at least once this week before the sunrise. Take a walk, or go somewhere that you can witness the dawning of a new day. In that moment, ask God to flood your life with the kind of light and life Christ brings.

- 🕊 Journal your experience. Write down your thoughts. Write down your prayer.

CLOSING PRAYER

We want to be open to the power of resurrection, God. Take our tentative commitment and encourage us with a vivid comprehension of your presence and your grace. Thank you for caring enough to enter our lives. Amen.

READINGS

Days 41–47

OPENING PRAYER

You entered Jerusalem on a donkey, Jesus, offering a kingdom of peace. Enter into our hearts and minds today, ride in majesty through the way that we live, tell your story through our relationships. We want to share the meal with you on Holy Thursday and we want to be there when you rise Easter morning. What we're the most nervous about is sharing your suffering on Good Friday. Grant us renewed commitment and fill us with your kind of love. Amen.

DISCUSSION QUESTIONS

- Imagine your personal story as a part of "The Greatest Story Ever Told." In what ways are you telling the story of Easter in your day-to-day life?

- Imagine a dinner party with friends. What would you want to share in the way of testimony if you knew it was your last meal together?

- The sign in the department store read, "Never has Easter been this cheap!" In what way is that a commentary on faith as well? What can we do to engage the story more seriously?

READING FROM "RIDING HIGH ON A DREAM."

"So let's go nuts today! Let's wave the branches and sing the songs! Let's not allow any of the small things to come between our great need and the life-giving affirmation of Jesus. We celebrate a Savior who rides into town on a donkey, because the way of the Cross is always the way that is unexpected."

- In what unexpected ways have you experienced Jesus this week?
- How do your inhibitions hold you back when you celebrate Jesus?
- How could you "Go nuts today" and honor Jesus?

PLAN

- Ask if you can wave a palm branch with the children, and join the parade!
- Plan to attend a Holy Thursday church event. If not, plan a dinner party with some friends where you can talk about your faith together and honor Christ in preparation for Good Friday.
- Begin each day of Holy Week with five minutes of meditative silence. Be deliberate and meditate on that day's scripture reading. Ask God to fill you with a deeper understanding of the Passion.

CLOSING PRAYER

This is the week we have been anticipating, Savior God. Guard our hearts and minds, keep us from distractions, speak to us through our spiritual practices, fill us with your love, and send us into the world with grace to share. Amen.

Session Eight

READINGS

Days 48–49

OPENING PRAYER

The tomb is empty! But the party has just got going! Thank you, Great God of Re-creation, for opening the door for us to participate in the work of salvation. Thank you for your amazing sacrifice, your awesome love, and your transcendent spirit of promise. Amen.

DISCUSSION QUESTIONS

- How, in your opinion (or your experience) is Easter Sunday a beginning rather than an ending of the celebration?

- How is your life different today because of your Lenten experience?

- What is one experience of joy that you have had over the past few days?

- Share one experience of God's felt presence since the last session.

- If Jesus has defeated death, what difference does that make in your life, today?

SCRIPTURE

Jesus answered, "My kingdom is not from this world. If my kingdom were from this world, my followers would be fighting to keep me from being handed over to the Jews. But as it is, my kingdom is not from here." Pilate asked him, "So you are a king?" Jesus answered, "You say that I am a king. For this I was born, and for this I came into the world, to testify to the truth. Everyone who belongs to the truth listens to my voice." John 18:36-37

- 🐦 Jesus spoke the phrase "But as it is, my kingdom is not from here." What idea is Jesus getting across to his listeners?

- 🐦 How is Christ's kingdom a reality in your experience?

- 🐦 When you hear Christ's voice, how does it make you feel as if you "belong to the truth"?

- 🐦 What part do you feel called to play in this kingdom Jesus is talking about?

POINT TO PONDER

The final reading, "Jesus as Destination and Guide" (p. 134), suggests that too many of us show up at church Sunday after Sunday as if we're visiting a grave, rather than celebrating an empty tomb! If the charge is true that we tend to keep Jesus in the tomb with the stone still rolled in place, what do we fear? And what do we plan to do about it?

CLOSING PRAYER

Thank you for being with us in this study, Resurrection God. Remain with us, we pray, as we live our faith out loud, as Eighth Day Believers. The implications of resurrection are huge, so help us to live in your light, animated by your life, and sustained by the Holy Spirit. We ask in the name of Jesus, who makes all this possible. Amen.